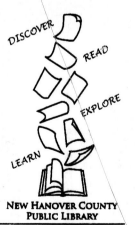

YEAR
of YES

SHONDA
RHIMES

SIMON & SCHUSTER

New York   London   Toronto   Sydney   New Delhi

Simon & Schuster
1230 Avenue of the Americas
New York, NY 10020

Some names and identifying characteristics have been changed, and some individuals are portrayed as composites. The timeline of certain events has been altered, with some events reordered, combined and/or compressed. The author is neither truly old nor is she truly a liar.

Quotations from *Grey's Anatomy* and *Private Practice* courtesy of ABC Studios.

First Simon & Schuster hardcover edition November 2015

SIMON & SCHUSTER and colophon are registered trademarks of Simon & Schuster, Inc.

For information about special discounts for bulk purchases, please contact Simon & Schuster Special Sales at 1-866-506-1949 or business@simonandschuster.com.

The Simon & Schuster Speakers Bureau can bring authors to your live event. For more information or to book an event contact the Simon & Schuster Speakers Bureau at 1-866-248-3049 or visit our website at www.simonspeakers.com.

Interior design by Ruth Lee-Mui

Manufactured in the United States of America

1   3   5   7   9   10   8   6   4   2

Library of Congress Cataloging-in-Publication Data
Rhimes, Shonda.
Year of yes / Shonda Rhimes. — First Simon & Schuster hardcover edition November 2015
    pages   cm
1. Rhimes, Shonda.   2. Television writers—United States—Biography.   I. Title.
    PN1992.4.R515A3 2015
    808.2'25—dc23
[B]   2015035684

ISBN 978-1-4767-7709-2
ISBN 978-1-4767-7714-6 (ebook)

For Harper, Emerson and Beckett,

May every year be a Year of *Yes*. May you inherit a future that no longer requires you to be an F.O.D. And if it is the future and that hasn't happened yet, go ahead and start the revolution. Mommy says you can.

and

For Delorse,

For giving me permission to start my own private revolution. And for saying yes to showing up every single time I've called your name. You are the F.O.D. within the family—the five of us who came behind you thank you for creating our second chances.

The need for change bulldozed a road
down the center of my mind.
—MAYA ANGELOU

If you want crappy things to stop
happening to you, then stop accepting
crap and demand something more.
—CRISTINA YANG, *GREY'S ANATOMY*

Hello

I'm Old and I Like to Lie
(A Disclaimer of Sorts)

I'm a liar.

And I don't care who knows it.

I make stuff up all the time.

Before you start speculating about my character and my sanity . . . let me explain myself. I make stuff up because I have to. It's not just something I like to do. I mean, I *do* like to do it. I thoroughly enjoy making stuff up. Fingers-crossed-behind-my-back flights of fancy make my motor run, shake my groove thing, turn me on.

I *do* like to make stuff up.

I *love* it.

It's also kind of ingrained in me. My brain? My brain naturally just leans in the direction of half truths; my brain turns toward fiction. Like a flower to the sun. Like writing with my right hand. Fabrication is like a bad habit that feels good, easy to pick up, hard to quit. Spinning tall tales, knitting yarns made of stories, is my dirty little vice. And I like it.

But it's not *just* a bad habit. I need to do it. I have to do it.

It turns out that making stuff up?

Is a job.

For real.

Seriously.

The very thing that had me on my knees in church during recess reciting the rosary for one nun or another at St. Mary's Catholic School in Park Forest, Illinois, is an actual honest-to-Jesus-Mary-and-Joseph job.

"Don't tell anyone, but my Mom? She escaped from Russia. She was engaged to this guy, Vladimir—she had to leave the love of her life behind and everything. It's so sad. And now she has to pretend she's a totally regular American or we could all be killed. Of *course* I speak Russian. *Dah.* What? She's *black* Russian, stupid. Like white Russian. But black Russian. Anyway, it doesn't matter what kind of Russian, we can never go there ever, she's a dead woman over there now. For trying to assassinate Leonid Brezhnev. What do you mean *why*? Don't you know anything? To stop nuclear winter. To save America. Duh."

You'd think I'd get extra credit for knowing who Leonid Brezhnev was. You'd think I'd get bonus points for reading up on Russian politics. You'd think someone would thank me for educating my fellow ten-year-olds about the Cold War.

Knees. Church. Nuns. Rosary.

I can recite the rosary in my sleep. I *have* recited the rosary in my sleep.

Making stuff up is responsible for that. Making stuff up is responsible for everything—everything I've done, everything I am, everything I have. Without the tales, the fiction, the stories I've spun, it is highly likely that right now, today, I'd be a very quiet librarian in Ohio.

Instead, the figments of my imagination altered whatever downward path the nuns at school expected my life to take.

The stuff I made up carried me from the small bedroom I shared with my sister Sandie in the suburbs of Chicago to an Ivy League dorm room in the hills of New Hampshire, and then it took me all the way to Hollywood.

My destiny rides squarely on the back of my imagination.

The sinful stories that earned me prayer as penance during recess are the same stories that now allow me to buy a bottle of wine plus a steak at the grocery store and not worry about the price. Being able to buy wine and steak and not think about the price is very important to me. It was a goal. Because when I was a struggling graduate student in film school, I often had no money. And so I often had to *choose* between wine and things like toilet paper. Steak did not even enter into the equation.

It was wine or toilet paper.

Wine.

Or.

Toilet paper.

The toilet paper did not always win.

Did I just see you give me a look? Was that . . . did you just *judge* me?

No. You are *not* about to come up into this book and judge me.

That is *not* how we are going to start off this journey. We are gonna ease on down the road. We're in this book together, my friend. So let she who is without wine cast the first stone. Otherwise . . .

Sometimes the toilet paper does not win.

Sometimes a broke woman needs the red wine more.

So you'll have to cut me some slack if I'm unapologetic about my love for the magic of a little bit of fibbing and invention.

Because I make stuff up for a living.

Imagining is now my job. I write television shows. I make up characters. I create whole worlds in my head. I add words to the lexicon of daily conversation—maybe you talk about your *vajayjay* and tell your friend that someone at work got *Poped* because of my shows. I birth babies, I end lives. I dance it out. I wear the white hat. I operate. I gladiate. I exonerate. I spin yarns and tell tall tales and sit around the campfire. I wrap myself in fiction. Fiction is my job. Fiction is it. Fiction is everything. Fiction is my *jam*.

Yes, I'm a liar.

But now I'm a *professional* liar.

Grey's Anatomy was my first real job in television. Having a show I created be my first real TV job meant that I knew nothing about working in TV when I began running my own show. I asked every TV writer I bumped into what this job was like, what being in charge of a season of a network television drama was like. I got loads of great advice, most of which made clear that every show was a very different, specific experience. With one exception: every single writer I met likened writing for television to one thing—laying track for an oncoming speeding train.

The story is the track and you gotta keep laying it down because of the train. That train is production. You keep writing, you keep laying track down, no matter what, because the train of production is coming toward you—no matter what. Every eight days, the crew needs to begin to prepare a new episode—find locations, build sets, design costumes, find props, plan shots. And every eight days after that, the crew needs to *film* a new episode. Every eight days. Eight days to prep. Eight days to shoot. Eight days, eight days, eight days, eight days. Which means every eight days, that crew needs a brand-new script. And my job is to damn well provide them with one. Every. Eight. Days. That train of production is a'coming. Every eight days that crew on that soundstage better have something to shoot. Because the worst thing you can do is halt or derail production and cost the studio hundreds of thousands of dollars while everyone waits. That is how you go from being a TV writer to being a failed TV writer.

So I learned to lay track quickly. Artfully. Creatively. But as fast as freaking lightning.

Lay some fiction on it.

Smooth some story into that gap.

Nail some imagination around those edges.

I always feel the heat of the speeding train on the backs of my thighs, on the heels of my feet, on my shoulder blades and elbows, on the seat of my pants as it threatens to run me down. But I don't step back and let the cool wind hit my face as I watch the train speed by. I never step back. Not because I can't. Because I don't want to. That is not the gig. And for me, there is no better gig on the face of the earth. The adrenaline, the rush, the . . . I call it the *hum*. There's a hum that happens inside my head when I hit a certain writing rhythm, a certain speed. When laying track goes from feeling like climbing a mountain on my hands and knees to feeling like flying effortlessly through the air. Like breaking the sound barrier. Everything inside me just shifts. I break the writing barrier. And the feeling of laying track changes, transforms, shifts from exertion into exultation.

I've gotten good at it, the making stuff up.

I could lie in the Olympics.

But there's another problem.

I am old.

Not shake-my-fist-and-holler-if-you-run-across-my-lawn old. And not revered-wrinkled-elder old. I'm not old on the outside. I mean, on the outside, I look *good*.

I look *young*.

I don't look old and probably never will. Seriously. I will never age. Not because I am a vampire or anything.

I will never age because I am my mother's child.

My mother? Looks incredible. At most, on a bad day, she looks like a slightly worried twenty-five-year-old who maybe partied a little too hard last night. I mean, the woman is nearing . . . she won't like it if I tell you. So let's just put it this way: my mother has six children, seventeen grandchildren and eight great-grandchildren. When I see her, I like to tell her that she is "keeping it tight." Mainly because it appalls her. Also because it makes her laugh. Mostly because we all know it's true. But secretly I say it because it's something of a relief to me—I know I've got that face to look forward to.

The women in my family? We've won the genetic lottery.

You think I'm kidding?

I'm not kidding.

When I get older, I will stand in line along with the rest of the women on my mother's side of the family and enjoy the benefits that come with cashing in that winning ticket. Because we didn't just win that lottery, we won the Powerball, baby. All six numbers—even the big red one.

My aunts, my cousins, my sisters . . . you should see us all standing around looking like toddlers in tiaras. We women, we descendants of my grandmother Rosie Lee? We look damn good. Our black don't crack—*for real*. As my sister Sandie and I like to remind each other, "We will always be the hottest women in the old folks' home."

And that is the thing that is so bittersweet and sad. Because my brain.

My brain. Oh, my brain.

My brain, she is old.

Really old.

Gumming-her-food old.

So, yes. Yes, I will be one of the two hottest women residing at the Sunset Senior Citizens Center for Old Folks Who Don't Want to Live Like *Grey Gardens*.

But while I most certainly will be a belle of that senior ball, I will not remember that I ever thought being hot in an old folks' home was a fun thing to be.

I may have won the genetic lottery on the outside, but on the inside . . .

We are choosing between wine and toilet paper up in here, okay?

My memory sucks.

It's subtle. Perhaps if I didn't spend my entire day needing to express myself, needing to pull words out of my head, I'd have never noticed it. But I do. So I did. Maybe if my first TV show hadn't been a medical show that sent me screaming to a doctor with hypochondriacal certainties of tumors and diseases every time I sneezed, I would shrug it off as lack of sleep. But it was. So I can't.

Names are forgotten, details of one event are switched with another, a crazy story I am sure was told by one friend was actually told by someone else. The insides of my brain are a fading photograph, stories and images drifting away to places unknown. Leaving patches of nothingness where a name or an event or a location should be.

Anyone who has watched *Grey's Anatomy* knows that I am obsessed with curing Alzheimer's. Anyone who knows me even vaguely knows that my greatest fear is getting Alzheimer's.

So I'm absolutely sure I have it. I'm *sure* I have Alzheimer's. So sure that I take my crappy memory and my shrieking hypochondria to the doctor.

I don't have Alzheimer's.

Yet.

(Thank you, universe. You are pretty and smart. So pretty and so smart.)

I don't have Alzheimer's.

I'm just old.

Pour one out for my youth.

Time is simply not my friend. My memory is ever-so-slowly being replaced by blank spaces. The details of my life are disappearing. The paintings are being stolen off the walls of my brain.

It's exhausting. And confusing. And sometimes funny. And often sad.

But.

I make stuff up for a living. Been doing it all my life. So.

Without ever committing to a plan, without ever actively trying, without even realizing it is going to happen, the storyteller inside me steps forward and solves the problem. My inner liar leaps in to take over my brain and begins to spin the yarns. Begins to just . . . fill in the blank spaces. To paint over the nothingness. To close the gaps and connect the dots.

To lay track for the train.

The train that is a'coming no matter what.

Because that's the gig, baby.

Putting fiction on it is where it is *at*.

Which leaves me with a conundrum.

This book is not fiction. It's not about characters that I made up. It doesn't take place at Seattle Grace or Pope & Associates. It's about me. It takes place in reality. It's supposed to be *just* the facts.

Which means I can't embellish. I can't add a little here or there. I can't put a bit of sparkly ribbon or a handful of glitter on it. I can't create a better ending or insert a more exciting twist. I can't just say screw it and go for the good story and say a rosary later.

I can't make stuff up. I need to tell you the truth. All I have to work with is the truth. But it's *my* truth. And therein lies the problem.

You get that, right?

So. This is my disclaimer, I suppose.

Is every single solitary word of this book true?

I hope so.

I think so.

I believe so.

But how in the hell would I remember if it wasn't?

I'm old.

I like to make stuff up.

Okay. It's possible. There could be some track in here. I could have laid track for the train all up in these pages. I didn't mean to. I didn't try to. I don't think I did. But it's possible.

I'll say this. This is the truth I remember. The truth as I know it. As much as an old liar can know. I'm doing my best. And so if I didn't get every detail correct, well . . .

. . . once more for the cheap seats, everybody . . .

I'm old.

And I like to lie.

Prologue

Full Frontal

When it was first suggested to me that I write about this year, my first instinct was to say no.

Writing about myself feels a lot like I have just decided to stand up on a table in a very proper restaurant, raise my dress and show everyone that I'm not wearing panties.

That is to say, it feels *shocking*.

It puts the bits of me that I usually keep to myself on display.

Naughty bits.

Secret bits.

See, I am an introvert. Deep. To the bone. My marrow is introvert marrow. My snot is introvert snot. Every cell in my body screams continuously at me with every word I type that writing this book is an unnatural act.

A lady never shows her soul outside the boudoir.

Showing you a bit of full-frontal *me* makes me nervous and twitchy, like I have a rash in an unfortunate place. It makes me breathe really hard in a weird panicked dog–sounding way. It makes me laugh inappropriately in public spaces whenever I think about people reading it.

Writing this book makes me uncomfortable.

And that, dear reader, is the point. It's the whole thing. Which is why I am writing it anyway. Despite the twitching and the laughing and the breathing.

Being too comfortable is what started all of this in the first place.

Well, being too comfortable plus hearing six startling words.

Plus turkey.

YEAR
of YES

1

NO

"You never say yes to anything."

Six startling words.

That's the beginning. That's the origin of it all. My sister Delorse said six startling words and changed everything. She said six words and now, as I write this, I have become a different person.

"You never say yes to anything."

She didn't even *say* the six startling words. She muttered them, really. Her lips barely moving, her eyes fixed intently on the large knife in her hands as she was dicing vegetables at a furious pace, trying to beat the clock.

yesyesyesyesyesyesyesyesyesyesyesyesyesyesyesyes

It's November 28, 2013.

Thanksgiving Day morning. So obviously, the stakes are high.

Thanksgiving and Christmas have always been my mother's domain. She has ruled our family holidays with flawless perfection. Food always delicious, flowers always fresh, colors coordinated. Everything perfect.

Last year, my mother announced that she was tired of doing all the work. Yes, she made it *look* effortless—that did not mean it *was* effortless. So, still reigning supreme, my mother declared she was abdicating her throne.

Now, this morning, is Delorse's first time stepping up to wear the crown.

This has made my sister intense and dangerous.

She doesn't even bother glancing up at me when she mutters the words. There is no time. Hungry family and friends will bear down on us in less than three hours. We have not even reached the turkey-basting segment of the cooking process. So unless my sister can kill me, cook me and serve me with stuffing, gravy and cranberry sauce, I am not getting her full attention right now.

"You never say yes to anything."

Delorse is the eldest child in our family. I am the youngest. Twelve years separate us; that age gap is filled by our brothers and sisters—Elnora, James, Tony and Sandie. With so many siblings between us, growing up, it was easy to feel as though the two of us existed in the same solar system but never visited each other's planets. After all, Delorse was heading off to college as I was entering kindergarten. I have vague childhood memories of her—Delorse cornrowing my hair way too tightly, giving me a braid headache; Delorse teaching my older brothers and sisters how to do a brand-new dance called The Bump; Delorse walking down the aisle at her wedding, my sister Sandie and me behind her holding up the train of her gown, our father at her side. As a child, she was the role model of the kind of woman I was supposed to grow up to be. As an adult, she's one of my best friends. Most of the important memories of my grown-up life include her. So I suppose it is fitting that she is here now, muttering these words at me. It is fitting that right now she's the one both telling me who I am supposed to grow up to be *and* standing at the center of what will become one of the most important memories of my life.

And this moment *is* important.

She doesn't know it. I don't know it. Not right now. Right now this moment doesn't feel important at all. Right now, this feels like Thanksgiving morning and she's tired.

She got up before dawn to call and remind me to take the twenty-one-pound turkey out of the refrigerator to settle. Then she drove the four blocks from her house to mine in order to do all the cooking for our big family dinner. It's not quite eleven a.m. but she's already been at it for hours. Chopping, stirring, seasoning. She's working really hard.

And I have been watching her.

It's not as bad as it sounds.

I'm not doing *nothing*.

I'm not *useless*.

I've been handing her things when she asks. Also, I have my three-month-old daughter strapped to my chest in a baby sling and my one-and-a-half-year-old daughter on my hip. I've combed my eleven-year-old's hair, turned off the TV show she was watching and forced a book into the child's hands.

And we're talking. My sister and I. We're talking. Catching up on all the things we have missed since, well . . . yesterday or maybe the day before.

Okay. Fine. *I'm* talking.

I'm talking. She's cooking. I'm talking and talking and *talking*. I have a lot to tell her. I'm listing for her all of the invitations that I've received in the last week or so. Someone wants me to speak at this conference and someone invited me to go to that fancy party and I've been asked to travel to such-and-such country to meet that king or to be on a certain talk show. I list ten or eleven invitations I received. I tell her about all of them in detail.

I will admit to you right now that I toss in a few extra juicy bits, spin a few tales, lay some track. I'm purposely boasting a little bit—I am trying to get a reaction out of my big sister. I want her to be impressed. I want her to think I'm cool.

Look, I was raised in a great family. My parents and siblings have many wonderful qualities. They are universally pretty and smart. And like I said, they all look like fetuses. But the members of my immediate family all share one hugely disgusting criminal flaw.

They do not give a crap about my job.

At all.

None of 'em.

Not a one.

They are frankly disturbed that anyone would be impressed by me. For any reason. People behaving toward me as though I might be vaguely interesting bewilders them deeply. They stare at one another, baffled, whenever someone treats me as anything other than what they know me to be—their deeply dorky, overly verbal, baby sister.

Hollywood is a bizarre place. It's easy to lose touch with reality here. But nothing keeps a person grounded like a host of siblings who, when someone requests your autograph, ask in a truly horrified tone, "Her? Shonda's autograph? Are you sure? Shonda? No wait, really, *Shonda*? Shonda *RHIMES*? *Why?*"

It's super rude. And yet . . . think of how many bloated egos would be saved if everyone had five older brothers and sisters. They love me. A lot. But they are not gonna stand for any celebrity VIP crap from the kid in Coke-bottle glasses they all saw throw up alphabet soup all over the back porch and then slip face-first in the vomit chunks.

Which is why right now I'm verbally tap-dancing around

the room, shaking it like I'm competing for a mirror-ball trophy. I'm trying to get my sister to show any sign of being impressed, a glimmer that she might think I'm remotely cool. Trying to get a reaction from these people I'm related to, well, it has almost become a game for me. A game I believe that one day I *will* win.

But not today. My sister doesn't even bother to blink in my direction. Instead, impatient, possibly tired and likely sick of the sound of my voice going on and on about my list of fancy invitations, she cuts me off.

"Are you going to do any of these things?"

I pause. A little taken aback.

"Huh?" That's what I say. "Huh?"

"These events. These parties, conferences, talk shows. Did you say yes to any of them?"

I stand there for a moment. Silent. Confused.

What is she talking about? Say yes?

"Well. No, I mean . . . no," I stammer, "I can't say . . . obviously I said no. I mean, I'm busy."

Delorse keeps her head down. Keeps chopping.

Later, when I think about it, I will realize she was probably not even listening to me. She was probably thinking about whether or not she had enough cheddar grated for the mac and cheese she had to make next. Or deciding how many pies to bake. Or wondering how she was going to get out of cooking Thanksgiving dinner next year. But in the moment, I don't get that. In the moment, my sister keeping her head down? It MEANS something. In the moment, my sister keeping her head down feels purposeful.

Deep.

Challenging.

Rude.

I have to defend myself. How do I defend myself? What do I—

At that exact moment (and this is so fortuitous I decide the universe *loves* me), Beckett, the sunny three-month-old baby strapped to my chest, decides to spit up a geyser of milk that runs down the front of my shirt in a creepy warm waterfall. On my hip, my prudish one-and-a-half-year-old, the moon to Beckett's sun, wrinkles her nose.

"I smell something, honey," she tells me. Emerson calls everyone "honey." As I nod at her and dab at the smelly hot milk stain, I pause. Take in the mess in my arms.

And I have my defense.

"Beckett! Emerson! I have babies!! *And* Harper! I have a tween! Tweens are delicate flowers! I can't just go places and do things!!! I have children to take care of!"

I holler this across the counter in my sister's general direction.

Wait. Speaking of taking care of stuff . . . I also have to take care of a little something called Thursday nights. Ha! I do a victory shimmy across the kitchen and point at her. Gloating.

"I also have a job! Two jobs! *Grey's Anatomy* AND *Scandal*! Three children and two jobs! I'm . . . busy! I am a mother! I'm a writer! I run shows!"

Bam!

I feel totally triumphant. I'm a mother. A *mother*, damn it. I have children. THREE children. And I'm running two television shows at one time. I have more than six hundred crew members depending on me for work. I'm a mother who works. I'm a working mother.

Like . . . Beyoncé.

Yes.

Exactly like Beyoncé.

I am bringing home the bacon AND frying it up in the pan. It's not an excuse. It's a fact. No one can argue with that. No one can argue with Beyoncé.

But I forgot that this is Delorse.

Delorse can argue with anyone.

Delorse puts down her knife. She actually stops cooking and puts down her knife. Then she raises her head to look up at me. My sister, the biggest winner in our family's genetic Powerball, is in her fifties. Late fifties. Her sons are grown men with degrees and careers. She has grandchildren. And yet I am often asked if my fifty-seven-year-old sister *is my child*.

The horror of it is sometimes too much.

So when she raises her head to look at me, she looks more

like a saucy fourteen-year-old than she does my eldest sibling. Her saucy-fourteen-year-old face eyes me.

"Shonda."

That's all she says. But it's said with such confidence . . .

So I blurt out—

"A *single* mother."

Now, that is shameless. You and I both know it. Because while the technical definition of "single mother" fits me—I am a mother, I am single—its cultural and colloquial meaning does not. Trying to appropriate that term as if I am a struggling mom doing my best to put food on the table makes me an ass. I know it. You know it. And unfortunately? Delorse also knows it.

I need to put an end to the conversation. I raise an eyebrow and make my bossy face. The one I make at the office when I need everyone to stop arguing with me.

My sister does not give a crap about my bossy face. But she picks up her knife again, goes back to chopping.

"Wash the celery," she tells me.

So I wash celery. Somehow the smell of fresh celery, the motion of the washing, Emerson's joy as she splashes the water over the counter, it all lulls me into a false sense of security.

Which is why I am not prepared.

I turn. Hand her the wet, clean celery. And I'm surprised when, still chopping, Delorse begins to speak.

"You are a single mother but you are not a *single mother*. I live four blocks away. Sandie lives four blocks away. Your parents live forty minutes away and would love to stay with the kids. You have literally the best nanny in the world. You have three amazing best friends who would step in and help at any time. You are surrounded by family and friends who love you, people who want you to be happy. You are your own boss—your job is only as busy as you make it. But you never do anything but work. You never have any fun. You used to have *so much fun*. Now, all of these amazing opportunities are coming your way—once-in-a-lifetime opportunities—and you aren't taking advantage of any of them. Why?"

I shift, uncomfortable. For some reason, I do not like this. I don't like anything about this conversation at all. My life is fine. My life is great. I mean, look around!

Look!

I'm . . . happy.

Ish.

I'm happyish.

Kind of.

Mind your own business, Delorse. You are annoying, Delorse. People aren't supposed to Benjamin Button so your face is clearly the result of a pact with Satan, Delorse! You know what, Delorse? You smell like poop.

But I don't say any of that. Instead I stand there for a long time. Watching her chop. And finally, I answer. Putting just the right amount of casual arrogance in my voice.

"Whatever."

And then I turn away, hoping to indicate that the conversation is over. I head over to the sitting area, where I gently settle an already napping Beckett into the bassinet. I place Emerson on the changing table for a fresh diaper. In a moment, I'll go upstairs and try to find a spit-up-free shirt to wear for dinner. The fresh diaper is on. I put Emerson on my hip, lay her head on my shoulder, and we swing back around to face my sister as I head for the stairs. That's when she says it. The six words.

Mutters them. Almost under her breath.

As she finishes chopping the onions.

Six startling words.

"You never say yes to anything."

For a single beat, time stops. Becomes a clear, frozen moment I'll never forget. One of the paintings that will never be taken from my mental wall. My sister, in a brown hoodie, her hair in a neat knot at the nape of her neck, standing there with that knife in her hand, head down, the little pile of white onion pieces on the cutting board before her.

She tosses the words out there.

"You never say yes to anything."

Tosses the words out there like a grenade.

You never say yes to anything.

Then my sister slides the onions over and begins chopping the celery. I head upstairs to change my shirt. Family and friends arrive. The turkey cooks perfectly. Dinner is delicious.

The grenade lies there in the middle of everything. Quiet. Camouflaged. I don't think about it.

You never say yes to anything.

Thanksgiving Day comes and goes.

2

Maybe?

The grenade sits dormant for several weeks.

It rolls around in my brain, the safety clip firmly in place. So quietly stealthy that I am able to forget it is there. I maintain my usual routine. I go to work, I write scripts, I work on episodes of TV, I come home, I snuggle babies, I read bedtime stories.

Life is normal.

One single out-of-the-ordinary event occurs: I fly to Washington as a new trustee of the Kennedy Center. I attend the celebrations, making my first trip to the White House. And then, for magical reasons that to this day I still don't understand, I am told I will be sitting with the president and the First Lady in their box at the Kennedy Center Honors.

I am not asked. I am told. I am not given a chance to say

no. Mainly because I am sure it never occurs to anyone that I would decline such an honor. Who would?

I wear a very beautiful black beaded evening gown. My date wears a new tuxedo. We sit right behind President and Mrs. Obama for the entirety of the ceremony. I am much too shy and nervous to croak out more than a few words when faced with a chance to speak to the actual president and First Lady. I certainly don't form sentences. But I enjoy myself. I have fun.

We drink cocktails in the same room as Carlos Santana and Shirley MacLaine. We get the street cred to be able to say we were there when Snoop Dogg thanked Herbie Hancock for creating hip-hop. We see Garth Brooks sing Billy Joel's "Goodnight Saigon" with a choir made up of veterans. It's amazing. The whole evening feels a bit enchanted. No matter how cynical the Beltway thinks it is or how world-weary politicians may seem, D.C. is a town that lacks the true cynicism of Hollywood. People actually get excited about things there and the enthusiasm is infectious. I fly back to Los Angeles filled with a buoyant sense of optimism.

The grenade explodes without warning.

It happens at four in the morning a few days before Christmas. I'm flat on my back in the middle of my king-size bed. Eyes pulled open against my will. Something's snapped me awake, yanked me out of sleep.

Being woken abruptly is not new.

Like every other mother on the planet, from the moment my first baby entered the house, I stopped getting real sleep. Motherhood means I'm always a little bit awake, a little bit alert at all times. One eye open. So being awakened by something in the middle of the night isn't surprising. What is surprising is that this something doesn't have anything to do with a furious kid standing in a crib screaming her head off. The house is silent. My girls are fast asleep.

So why am I awake?

If they had asked me, I would have said no.

That thought makes me sit up in bed.

What?

If they had asked me, I would have said no.

My face gets hot. I'm embarrassed, as if there is someone else in the room hearing the words inside my brain.

If they had asked me if I wanted to sit in the presidential box at the Kennedy Center Honors, I would have said no.

Ridiculous.

But it's true. It's clearly true.

I am as sure of this as I am of the need to breathe. I would have said no carefully. Respectfully. Graciously. I would have come up with a creative excuse, expressed both extreme honor and regret. The excuse would have been good, the excuse would have been *brilliant*.

I mean, come on.

I'm a writer. I would have been eloquent and delightful—no one can decline an invitation as beautifully as I can. You're all amateurs at bailing on something; I bail on events so well that I can do it in the major leagues.

I nod to myself. Certain. However I handled it, I definitely would have said no. That is an unquestionable fact.

If they had asked, I would have said no.

Seriously?

I am up and out of bed. Sleep doesn't have a chance now. This requires thought. This requires wine. Downstairs, I throw myself on my sofa and stare at the lights of my Christmas tree. Glass of wine in hand, I drink about the question.

Why would I have said no?

But I know the answer. I knew the answer before I got out of bed. I just wanted the wine.

Because it's scary.

I would have said no to sitting in the presidential box at the Kennedy Center with POTUS and FLOTUS because the prospect of saying yes was terrifying to me.

I would have said no because if I had said yes, I would have had to actually *do* it. I would have had to actually go and sit in the box and be there to meet the president and the First Lady. I would have had to make small talk and say things. I would have had to drink cocktails near Carlos Santana.

I would have had to do all of the things that I, in fact, *did do* that night.

And I had a wonderful time. When all was said and done, it was one of the most memorable nights of my life.

Look, I am known for giving good story.

The kind of good story told over dinner that makes my friends laugh, that gets my date to accidentally spit his cocktail across a table. The kind of good story that has everyone asking me to "tell that one again." That's my superpower—telling good stories. Smooth stories. Funny stories. Epic stories.

I can make any story good. I can take the lamest tale and make it compelling. The thing is, a good story is not about purposely lying. The best stories are true. Giving good story just requires that I . . . leave out the untidy bits.

The bits where, before I leave for the White House, I spend ten minutes convincing myself that I do not have the stomach flu, that I am fine. Where I consider licking the dust at the bottom of the Xanax bottle because oh yeah, I don't *take* Xanax anymore, it's been twelve years since Xanax was my friend. *Yuck, this Xanax dust is twelve-year-old Xanax dust?*

Where I sleep for fourteen hours straight because I am so numb with stress that it's either sleep or run. And I don't mean jog on a treadmill. I mean, run. I mean, get in a car, go to the airport, get on a plane and run away.

Run.

That seems like a much better plan than going out in public with every nerve ending in my body screaming.

This is who I am.

Silent.

Quiet.

Interior.

More comfortable with books than new situations.

Content to live within my imagination.

I've lived inside my head since I was a kid. My earliest memories are of sitting on the floor of the kitchen pantry. I stayed there for hours in the darkness and warmth, playing with a kingdom I created out of the canned goods.

I was not an unhappy kid. Because I was the baby in a family of eight, at any given moment, someone was available to read to me, applaud whatever story I had come up with or let me listen in on their teenage secrets. The end to every sibling argument over the extra cookie or the last slice of cake was always an egalitarian sigh: "Give it to the baby."

I was loved, I was a star, I was the Blue Ivy of my world. I was not an unhappy kid.

I was just an unusual kid.

Lucky for me, my parents held the unusual in high regard. And so when I wanted to play with the cans in the pantry for hours on end, my mother didn't tell me to stop messing around with the food and go somewhere else to play. Instead, she declared it a sign of creativity, closed the pantry door and let me be.

You have her to thank for my love of long-form serialized drama.

The world I created inside the small closet filled with canned goods and cereal was serious; these days I would describe it as a winter-is-coming-where-are-my-dragons kind of solo play date, but this was not HBO. This was the suburbs in the 1970s. We didn't need reality TV because TV was *real*. Nixon was going down. As Watergate played out on the tiny black and white set my mother had dragged into the kitchen and balanced on a chair just outside the pantry doors, my three-year-old imagination made a world of its own. The big cans of yams ruled over the peas and green beans while the tiny citizens of Tomato Paste Land planned a revolution designed to overthrow the government. There were hearings and failed assassination attempts and resignations. Every once in a while, my mom would open the pantry door, flooding my world with light. She'd politely tell me she needed vegetables for dinner. The canned judiciary would sentence a can of corn to death for treason and I'd deliver the guilty party into the hands of the executioner.

Man, that pantry was fun.

You see the problem? Did you *read* the problem?

Man, that pantry was fun.

That just came out of my mouth. I actually said it aloud WHILE I typed it. And I said it without any irony. I said it with a big dorky wistful grin on my face.

I had a wonderful childhood, but I lived so deep in my imagination that I was happier and more at home in that pantry with the canned goods than I ever was with people. I felt safer in the pantry. Freer in that pantry. True when I was three years old.

And somehow even *more* true at forty-three.

As I sit on my sofa staring into the Christmas lights, I realize that I would still be partying in my pantry if I thought I could get away with it. If I didn't have children who needed me to be in the world. I fight the instinct every day. Which is why I now have a garden for vegetables.

If they had asked, I would have said no.

I would have said no.

Because I always say no.

And that's when the grenade explodes.

Suddenly it's Thanksgiving and I'm back in that kitchen, covered in spit-up, watching my sister chop those onions. And I understand her now.

You never say yes to anything.

I don't just understand her—*I believe her*. I hear her. And I know. She is right.

BOOM.

Grenade.

When the dust settles and everything is clear, I am left with one thought rattling through my head.

I'm miserable.

That makes me put down my wineglass. Am I drunk? Am I *kidding* me? Did I just think that?

Honestly, I'm a little indignant with myself. I'm embarrassed to even be having that thought. I'm ashamed, if you really wanna know. I'm bathed in shame.

I'm miserable?

I'm still a little ashamed to be telling you that right now.

I'm miserable.

Who in the hell do I think I am?

A whiner. That's who. A great big old whiner person.

You know who gets to be miserable? Malala. Because *someone shot her in the face.* You know who else? The Chibok schoolgirls. Because the terrorist group Boko Haram kidnapped them from school for forced marriage (which is just like regular marriage except exactly the opposite and full of rape) and *no one cares anymore.* You know who else? Anne Frank. Because she and about six million other Jewish people were murdered by Nazis. And? Mother Teresa. Because everyone else was too lazy to treat the lepers and so she had to do it.

It's pretty shameful of me to sit around saying I'm miserable when there are no bullets in my face and no one's kidnapped me or killed me or left me alone to treat all the lepers.

I grew up in a family where hard work was not optional. My parents worked very hard to raise and educate six—count 'em, *six*—children. And at some point, it dawned on me that the reason I had such a great childhood and never wanted for anything was because my parents worked extremely hard so we could have crazy things like food and gas and clothes and tuition. In high school, I got a job scooping ice cream at Baskin-Robbins and I have had a job ever since. So I am very aware that these days I live in a rarefied world. I know that I am extremely fortunate. I know that I have incredible children, a fantastic family, great friends, a spectacular job, a lovely home and all my arms, legs, fingers, toes and organs intact. I know I don't have the right to complain. Not about my life in comparison to anyone else's life. Unless that anyone is Beyoncé.

Damn, my life is so bad next to Beyoncé's life. So is yours. *Everyone's* life is so bad next to hers. If you know otherwise, if you know that Beyoncé's life is terrible for some reason, please, do not come up to me on the street and correct me. I need to believe that Beyoncé's life is perfect. It keeps me going.

But except for Beyoncé, I know how fortunate I am. I have no delusions that I am suffering in any real, true way. And so it *does* embarrass me to say it. I mean, you don't hear Malala complaining.

But you know why you don't hear Malala complaining?

Because Malala and her spiritual buddies Mother Teresa and Anne Frank are all MUCH better people than I am. Obviously. Because I'm clearly a giant whining baby and I suck. Because in that predawn, staring at my Christmas lights, even though I am ashamed, I cannot avoid it. The realization feels like plunging into an icy lake:

I am miserable.

Admitting this takes my breath away. I feel as though I am revealing new information to myself. Learning a secret I've been keeping from myself.

I am miserable.

Truly, deeply unhappy.

In December 2013, I was incredibly successful. I had two hugely popular television shows on the air—*Grey's Anatomy* and *Scandal*—and had just retired a third, *Private Practice*. My company, Shondaland, was in the midst of working with writer Peter Nowalk to develop a show that would soon become our newest hit, *How to Get Away with Murder*. So yeah, from the outside, I think everything probably looked great. And as long as I was writing, as long as my fingers were on the keyboard, as long as I was at Seattle Grace or Pope & Associates, as long as I was laying track and feeling the *hum* in my brain . . . I was fine. I was happy.

I know that I certainly tried to project the idea that my life was perfect. And I tried not to think about it too hard.

I went to work. I worked a lot. I came home. I spent time with my kids. I spent time with the guy I was dating. I slept.

That's it.

In public, I smiled. A lot. I did a HUGE amount of smiling. And I did what I called "Athlete Talk." Athlete Talk is what happens on all of those interviews that take place right after any pro sports event you see on TV. A boxing match or an NBA game. Serena Williams smashing some record in tennis. Olympic swimming.

Good Athlete Talk is when the athlete goes before the press and keeps a smile on her face, voice bland and pleasant as she deftly fields one reporter's question after the other—never once saying anything of controversy or substance. My favorite Athlete Talker of all time is Michael Jordan. He'd stand there after scoring 5,635 points in one game, sweat pouring down his head, towering over some tiny reporter:

"I'm just happy to be playing the game of basketball," he'd say, smiling.

But, Michael, how do you feel about famine, politics, the WNBA, cartoons, Hanes underwear, tacos, anything?

"I'm thrilled to do what I can for the ball club. The Bulls are home to me," he'd chuckle pleasantly. And then he'd amble away. Presumably to the locker room, where he stopped being a Good Athlete Talker and started being a PERSON.

I was a Good Athlete Talker that year.

"I am just happy to be working for ABC."

"It's not my job to question my time slot. My job is to make the shows."

"I'm proud to be a part of the ABC team."

"I'm thrilled to do what I can for the network. ABC is home to me."

"I'm just happy to be playing the game of basketba—I mean, writing for TV."

And it was true. I was happy and proud and thrilled. I did like ABC. (I still do. Hello, ABC!) Just as I'm sure Michael truly liked the Bulls. But that Athlete Talk didn't have anything to do with liking my job.

It had to do with staying inside the pantry.

Keeping that door shut. Hearing Nixon on the outside. Only reaching one arm out into the sliver of light to hand out peas or corn or yams. Giving the people what they wanted. Then closing that door again.

Any actual parts of me, anything real, anything human, anything honest, I kept to myself. I was a very good girl. I did what everyone needed me to do.

And at the end of every day, as a reward, I poured myself a glass of red wine.

Red wine was joy in Shondaland.

yesyesyesyesyesyesyesyesyesyesyesyesyesyesyesyes

I used to be a really happy person. A *vibrant* person. I may have been shy and introverted but I had a rowdy, fun crowd of friends, some of whom I'd known since college and, with them around me, I was dance-on-the-tables Shonda, drive-to-New-Orleans-at-a-moment's-notice Shonda, adventurous-and-always-up-for-anything Shonda. Where did she go?

I had no real way to account for my unhappiness. For once, the storyteller had nothing to tell. I had no idea *why* I was unhappy, no specific moment or reason to point to. I just knew it was true.

Whatever that spark is that makes each one of us alive and unique . . . mine had gone. Stolen like the paintings on the wall. The flickering flame responsible for lighting me up from the inside, making me glow, keeping me warm . . . my candle had been blown out. I was shut down. I was tired. I was afraid. Small. Quiet.

The lives of my characters had become unimaginably huge. People all over the world knew Meredith and Olivia. At the same time, my life had so drained of color and excitement that I could barely see it.

Why?

You never say yes to anything.

Oh yeah. That.

I put down the glass of wine and lay on the sofa. And really thought about those six words.

You never say yes to anything.

Maybe it was time to start saying yes.

Maybe.

3

Umm, Yes . . . ?

January 13 is my birthday.

Yippee.

I love birthdays.

Because I love birthday parties.

When I found out there was something called a Puppy Party? Where they bring PUPPIES for kids to hold and cuddle for an hour and it's not puppy abuse, it's good for the puppies because they are training the puppies to be service dogs? I almost lost my mind jumping up and down. Puppies! A party with puppies! COME ON! That exists?

I like puppy parties and face painters and candy buffets and that guy with a guitar singing silly songs and ice cream and even some (very few, non-scary) clowns. And if you are past the age where helium balloons and face painting get you so excited and/or terrified that there's a danger you will pee your pants, I like dance parties and costume parties and dinner parties and seventies disco parties. I'm a firm believer that parties make everything better.

You'd think a shy person would hate birthday parties. I love them. Small parties and big parties. I don't necessarily love to *attend* them but I love the magic of them. I love the *idea* of them. I love to hug the corners of the walls and watch the good times. I love being with friends.

But today? This birthday?

I get out of the shower and lean really close to the bathroom mirror. So close I can see all my pores. Then I glare at my face.

"So you made it out of a uterus a long time ago. Big deal," I whisper. "So did *everybody else* on the planet. What else you got?"

Then I think about going back to bed.

Really. I usually *love* my birthday. I do. But today, I am nervous. Edgy. I feel prickly and strange. Like everyone is looking at me. I'm unnerved. There's a pit of something odd in my stomach.

It's the same feeling I used to have waking up with a hangover back in my twenties. I'd lie in bed, waiting for the bed to stop spinning. Wondering WHY I ever thought seven cocktails was a good idea. Feeling that same pit of oddness in my belly. In my gut. And I'd wait, every synapse on patrol—*we're on high alert, soldier, this is not a drill*—for the wave of memory to wash over me. To spill over my brain in a cascade of shame as I remembered whatever crazy thing it was I'd done the night before.

I slept with WHO?

I cried WHERE?

I sang WHAT song?

This birthday morning, that's what it feels like. A hangover morning. Except without all the bloaty puffy fun of the cocktails.

I promised myself that I would do WHAT?

Downstairs, wearing a birthday hat made by the kids, I eat cake for breakfast. I consume almost the entire cake by myself. And I do not feel bad about it. The cake is everything to me. I want to have this cake's babies. I savor each bite. I am like a death row inmate having her last meal.

In a text to one of my closest friends that day, I write the following:

"Am going to say yes to anything and everything that scares me. For a whole year. Or until I get scared to death and you have to bury me. Ugh."

My friend writes back:

"Holy crap."

I am not enthusiastic. But I am determined. My logic is wildly simple. It goes like this:

- Saying no has gotten me here.
- Here sucks.
- Saying yes might be my way to someplace better.
- If not a way to someplace better, at least to someplace different.

I didn't have a choice. I didn't *want* a choice. Once I saw the unhappiness, felt the unhappiness, recognized and named it . . . well, just knowing about it made me itchy. Like itchy on the inside of my brain. Continuing to say no was not going to get me anywhere at all. And standing still was no longer an option. The itchy was too much. Besides, I am not a person who can see a problem and *not* solve it.

Before you start to praise me (and frankly, I don't see how you possibly could at this point—but just in case), I want to be clear: I know that I said that I am not a person who can see a problem and not solve it. But I don't mean that in a "heroic Rosa Parks refuses to give up her seat on the bus" way. I mean it in a sad, control-freak, "the toast crusts must be cut off to the same exact millimeter measurement every time" way. Meaning I'm not easygoing about these things.

That's not how I'm built.

That's not how any type A, obsessive, workaholic control freak is built.

Obviously.

I'm a doer.

I do.

So. When I say I'm going to do something, I do it. When I say I'm going to do something, I *really* do it. I throw myself into it and I *do*. I do my *ass* off. I do right up to the finish line. No matter what.

No.

Matter.

What.

This is all made worse by the fact that I'm competitive. Not normal-people competitive. Not friendly competitive. Scary-psychotic competitive. Never hand me a volleyball. Don't ask me to play a fun hand of cards. I have never heard of a casual round of Scrabble. We started a bake-off at *Grey's Anatomy* and I had to remove myself from the competition. Something about it maybe being kind of a little bit like workplace harassment when I forced my writing staff to bake in competition against one another. And maybe it was also not so good when I performed a touchdown dance during the medal ceremony while yelling, "IN YOUR FACE, BITCHES!!!!" at whoever placed behind me.

Like I said, I'm competitive.

I'm not invited to *anyone's* game night.

Look. I'm a person who goes all in.

I lean in. I *lean all the way in*. I lean so far in that sometimes I'm lying down.

Hell, I don't own Thursday nights for *nothing*.

I tell you this so that you understand how big this yes-for-a-year thing was for me. This Year of Yes thing was gigantic. The Year of Yes promise was a commitment. A binding contract between me and my greatest competitor and judge—me. Backing out would mean months of self-flagellation and plummeting self-esteem. I would talk about me like a *dog*. Things would get ugly.

Also, honestly?

I was just . . . desperate.

Something had to change. It had to. Because this couldn't be it.

Having it all.

This could not possibly be what having it all was supposed to feel like. Could it? Because if it was, if *this* is what I spent all this time and energy working so hard for, if this was what the promised land looked like, was what success felt like, was what I sacrificed for . . .

I didn't even want to consider it. So I wouldn't. I would not think about that. Instead, I would look ahead, take a deep breath and just . . . believe. Believe that the road continued. Believe that there was more.

I would believe and I would say yes.

I told myself that and then I ate that whole cake and drank four mimosas while trying to believe.

yesyesyesyesyesyesyesyesyesyesyesyesyesyesyesyes

A week later, the phone rings at my Shondaland office. President Hanlon from Dartmouth College is calling. College presidents do not make it a habit to telephone me. I have met President Hanlon, a very nice man, exactly once. Nevertheless, here he is, President Hanlon of Dartmouth College, on my phone. Calling. He has a question. He wants to know if I will give the commencement speech at the college's graduation in June.

A twenty-minute speech. In front of about ten thousand people.

Ummm.

Universe?

Are you freaking kidding me?

There is an actual full minute that occurs on that phone call in which no air moves in or out of my lungs. President Hanlon may or may not be speaking. I do not know because the roar in my ears is making it impossible for me to hear.

Say yes to everything for a year.

This is it. It's happening. And now that it is here, saying yes stops being just a vague idea. Now the reality of what I am embarking upon sends my brain thundering around inside of my skull.

Say yes?

There's no way to plan. There's no way to hide. There's no way to control this. Not if I am saying yes to everything.

Yes to everything scary.

Yes to everything that takes me out of my comfort zone.

Yes to everything that feels like it might be crazy.

Yes to everything that feels out of character.

Yes to everything that feels goofy.

Yes to everything.

Everything.

Say yes.

Yes.

Speak. Speak NOW.

"Yes," I say. "Yes."

President Hanlon and I chat some more. I think it's pleasant. I think I'm calm. I really have no idea. I am focused on breathing in and out. On lowering the roar I hear. When I hang up the phone, I consider what I've done.

Speech. Commencement. Ten thousand people.

I input the date into my calendar.

June 8, 2014.

June.

That's about six months away. Six months is pretty far off.

Six months is a *lifetime*.

Okay. I shrug and go back to writing my *Grey's Anatomy* script notes.

Relieved. Not a big deal. I'll think about it later.

I file it away in the back of my brain and forget about it. I forget about it for *five and a half months*. You'd think that would be bad, given the giant speech I have to write. But instead, it turns out to be lucky. It turns out that I have other hurdles.

The Dartmouth commencement speech is technically my first yes.

Really, though?

The Dartmouth commencement speech is the first thing I say yes *to*. But it's not the first yes that I actually have to DO.

That's a different yes. And that yes? Turned out to be something much more terrifying.

Hello, Jimmy Kimmel.

4

Yes to the Sun

"They want you to be on *Kimmel*."

My publicist, Chris DiIorio, is talking to me.

Yeah, I have a publicist. A publicist sounds like an "I'm on the cover of *Vogue*" kind of thing to have. The kind of thing you have if you are luminous like Jennifer Lawrence or stop traffic every time you move like Lupita Nyong'o.

As I write this, my hair is standing straight up on my head because it's been a few days since I combed it and I'm wearing a pair of pajamas where the top and bottom do not match. They're not even the same fabric. The bottoms are silky, the top is stretch knit. There's a hole in the knee of the pajamas. Hello, *Vogue*. Yeah, I have a publicist.

When I first got a publicist, I told him and his team that my main reason for having a publicist was so that I never ever had to do any publicity. Everyone thought this was a joke. I was not joking.

It seems, being that everyone around me knows that I am awkward, introverted and visibly uncomfortable when meeting new people, that it would be kinda obvious that I would be panicked at the thought of standing on a stage talking to an audience, having my photo taken by a horde of photographers, being on TV, making public appearances of any kind, really.

You'd get that it would probably not be my favorite thing, right? You would, gentle reader, wouldn't you?

That is because you don't work in Hollywood.

In Hollywood, it is assumed that a person would be excited about a spotlight shining right on their face while they sat on a toilet on live TV.

I joke, right? No, still not joking.

Seriously. I think, given the chance, there are plenty of people in Hollywood who would LINE UP to do it. They'd line up for a casting session that read "PERSON ON TOILET."

Why? WHY?

For the exposure. For the *endorsement* opportunity.

"I could have my own line of toilets, you never know," they'd say, and plop right down on that porcelain throne.

When I meet you, let's hold hands and weep for humanity, okay?

The terrifying existence of willing public-toilet-sitters in this town is why my publicist, Chris, is genuinely confused when I say I never want any publicity. He tells me that I will change my mind.

In the words of the greatest singer ever, Whitney Houston, on the greatest reality show that ever was, *Being Bobby Brown*: "*Hell to the naw.*"

Even if I *was* Beyoncé, even if I woke up like *that*? I would still prefer to stay hidden. I would still want to quietly write scripts back there in the corner where no one could see me. I *never* want anyone looking at me. Being looked at makes me nervous.

When I am required by ABC to do publicity, I often feel (and, sadly, look) like Bambi's mother—right before the hunter shoots her. Her head snapped up, ears cocked, eyes wide, all freaked out . . .

It's not an attractive look.

At Dartmouth, I acted in some plays for a student theater group named BUTA. I enjoyed it. I sort of reveled in it. I was even mildly decent at it. I got compliments. But I wasn't me. I never had to step in front of an audience as Shonda Rhimes. My own words and thoughts were not needed. I just said whatever Ntozake Shange or George C. Wolfe or Shakespeare told me to say. No one was looking at *me*. They were looking through me to the writers. I never felt I was visible onstage.

Back then, I had fun in front of an audience. But now? It

didn't matter the venue or the medium. Now, it was always akin to torture. And season after season, the TCAs were a prime torture method.

Every year, twice a year, all the cable and network channels host a weeklong event for TV critics called, quite simply, TCAs. It's a chance for the critics to talk to actors, show-runners, directors. More times than I can count, ABC has requested my presence on a TCA panel.

Onstage doing a panel at TCAs, I know I always looked fine. In fact, I looked stern—like a scolding schoolmarm. I've seen all the photos. I'm frowning, stony. I am actually amazed by my face's ability to not betray my inner turmoil. The extreme fear seemed to freeze my face, turning me into a statue to protect me while onstage.

But beforehand, every single time, before I got to the stage . . . there was mumbling, there was sweating, there was shaking. There was the makeup artist charged with reapplying the mascara that washed off my face after the silent thirty-second crying jag required to quell my rising hysteria. There were executives from ABC who gathered around to say encouraging things as I paced back and forth, my glassy eyeballs spinning with fear. And then there was the exquisite bottle of red wine always given to me by the network president, who owned a vineyard. Because I never *ever* spoke in public without two glasses of wine in my system. Nature's beta blocker.

I am not saying that it was right.

I am saying that it *worked*.

My only good memory of sitting on that TCA stage was the year *Desperate Housewives* creator Marc Cherry very kindly took pity on me during a showrunners' panel. As a storm of questions about an unhappy actress came my way, he jumped in, answering and deflecting the worst of them with a series of amazing jokes. Twenty minutes before, someone— I don't remember who—had been forced to pry my fingers off the door handle of my car to get me inside. I hadn't been resisting. I'd just been frozen by fear and unable to move.

I was a walking panic attack. My stage fright was so complete and overwhelming that it ruled my every public appearance. Award acceptance speeches, interviews, talk shows . . . Oprah.

Oprah.

I have been interviewed by Oprah three times.

Here is what I remember about being interviewed by Oprah.

A white-hot flashing light behind my eyes. A strange numbness in my limbs. A high-pitched buzzing sound in my head.

So, y'know . . . nothing.

NOTHING.

I am from the suburbs of Chicago. I was *raised* on Oprah. I was watching *The Oprah Winfrey Show* when it was called

AM Chicago. I bought everything she told us to buy and read every book she told us to read. I took notes on every word of wisdom she shared with us through the television. I was baptized Catholic but I was Church of Oprah. If you are a person on the planet, you know what I am talking about. Everybody knows. It's OPRAH.

Being interviewed by Oprah was no small thing for me.

What do I remember about these precious moments spent with her?

Nothing.

The *O* magazine interview? Nothing.

The Oprah show interview with the cast of *Grey's Anatomy*? Zilch.

The *Oprah's Next Chapter* interview with Kerry Washington? Not a damn thing.

I do have vivid memories of the moments just *before* these interviews. That first time, *Grey's* costume designer Mimi Melgaard smoothed my skirt and spun me around, checking to make sure I looked okay. Then she nodded with approval and pointed a firm finger at me.

"Do not move until you see Oprah."

She didn't have to tell me that.

I couldn't have moved if I'd wanted to. I stood in the doorway of my office. Swaying very slightly back and forth. My feet already hurting in their very first pair of Manolo Blahniks.

My mind was as blank as a baby chicken.

I felt a layer of sweat wash over me. *Sweat.* Robotically, I began raising and lowering my arms, hoping to keep giant circular pit stains from appearing and ruining all of Mimi's Pygmalion work.

Raise and lower, raise and lower, raise and lower . . .

Flapping. I was flapping my arms.

Now I looked like a baby chicken.

It didn't matter. The rising terror thundering through me was growing louder and louder, taking me somewhere so far past fear that I felt almost . . . serene. It was like listening to a sound so high-pitched that your eardrums cease to be able to process it and the sound becomes silent. My screaming fear was so loud that it was silent.

The baby chicken was losing its head.

I watched as Oprah's black SUV rumbled onto the studio lot. I watched as Oprah's black SUV rolled into the VIP parking space. I watched as first one woman and then a second woman climbed from the black SUV. The first woman so recognizable, so familiar, that I literally only had to see the tip of her foot hitting the ground to know—it was Oprah. But the second woman . . . still flapping my sweaty arms, I stared. I couldn't identify the second woman. Who was it?

And then the arm flapping stopped.

Gayle, my brain realized. *That is Gayle. Sweet Mother of Television, I am looking at both Oprah AND Gayle.*

And that is the last thing I remember before the nothing-ness of terror stole all the fun away from me.

"How was it?" My sisters Sandie and Delorse grilled me breathlessly on the phone later that evening. The ONE time I managed to impress my sisters. The one time, and—

I. Don't. Know.

That is *not* what I said.

Have you learned nothing about me since starting this book? No, you have. You know me. You *know*.

I'm old. And I like to lie.

I did what I'd always done. Once Oprah got back in her SUV and drove away, I spent hours wandering around, casu-ally asking anyone who'd witnessed even a second of Oprah-ness all about it. Getting them to recap what they saw. It was a coping mechanism that had always worked for me. I was careful about it. Because when you go around asking people to tell you about yourself, you sound like kind of a jerk.

"Hey, tell me what I said. What was I like? Was I funny? Was I interesting? Tell me more about me talking to Oprah. Was it good?"

It's one thing for people to know you are nervous and have stage fright. They are sympathetic to that. But how do you admit to people that you don't remember the biggest in-terview of your career? That is weird. You know what people would say about that? I'll tell you. People would say:

Drugs.

So I kept my mouth shut.

It was the worst with Oprah. My admiration and fear merged into some sort of fireball of terror, so that the paintings were not just stolen off the walls of my brain but burned down to a heap of ashes. Never to be recovered.

With everyone else, I stood a chance. A small chance. But to some degree, all the interviewers were scary. Every talk show was a blur. Every interview went the same way. Down the drain.

yesyesyesyesyesyesyesyesyesyesyesyesyesyesyesyes

I've been asked to be on *Kimmel* before.

It makes sense that Jimmy Kimmel would want people from my shows on his show. Because of the ratings. My TGIT shows (that's how ABC promotes my Thursday night lineup of shows—"Thank God It's Thursday") get good ratings. Good ratings are good for everyone. Here's why: my good ratings mean that when actors who star on my shows are guests on *Jimmy Kimmel Live* (also on ABC), it's great for Jimmy's ratings too. What's great for us is great for Jimmy.

This is what is called *synergy*. I know this because people say this word to me a lot. Then they give me meaningful looks.

"Synergy." Meaningful look. I nod and smile, but between you and me? I think *synergy* sounds like the word one uses to define the calories two people burn off during sex.

Think about it.

*Syn*ergy.

Anyway.

It turns out that Jimmy, who is a truly hilarious person, a very nice guy and a great talk show host, doesn't just like us for our ratings. He actually really likes our shows. I *think* he does anyway. He definitely likes the casts of our shows. This year, he especially seems to love the cast of *Scandal*. Which is just fine because the cast of *Scandal* loves Jimmy and they enjoy being on his show.

And so each Thursday, actors like Kerry Washington and Katie Lowes get dressed up and pay Jimmy and his studio audience a visit. They come back and tell me stories. They tell me how much fun it is to be on Jimmy's show. They tell me about the skits they do. The pranks they pull. The jokes they tell. It sounds fun. And when I watch it all on *Jimmy Kimmel Live* on TV late at night, it LOOKS fun.

Yay for everyone!

But for some reason, Jimmy now wants something more. For some reason, he wants me to be a guest on his show.

Jimmy likes this idea.

ABC likes this idea.

My publicist likes this idea.

I do not like this idea.

No one cares.

No one *believes* me.

Because who doesn't want to be on TV?

Quick, everyone climb on that toilet and roll camera!

This year, Jimmy's people (every show has "people"—Kimmel's are extraordinarily nice) have asked a few times if I will be a guest on his show.

"They want you to be on *Kimmel*."

My publicist, Chris. Talking to me. We're on the phone. Which is lucky for me because of the jail time that comes with assault.

"You mean," I say tightly, "*Jimmy Kimmel LIVE*."

"Uh-huh." He sounds nonchalant. Casual. But he knows.

He knows how I feel about publicity. He knows how I feel about being interviewed. He knows how I feel about being interviewed on TV. And he especially knows how I feel about *live* TV.

You know what happens on live TV?

Janet Jackson's Super Bowl Boob happens on live TV. Adele Dazeem happens on live TV. President Al Gore happens on live TV.

You know what else happens on live TV?

Shonda walking out to greet Jimmy and instead of walking like a *normal* person, I trip over my own feet, falling and cracking my head on the corner of Jimmy's desk, causing my cerebrospinal fluid to leak out as I lie twitching on the ground with my dress bunched up around my waist, revealing my double Spanx to a national audience.

Shonda, under the hot lights of the studio and massively overcome by nerves, sweating so profusely that tsunamis of water roll down my face in a hideous but fascinating car-crash way that no one can look away from until finally, dehydrated from the water loss, I simply end the misery by fainting on the floor in front of Jimmy's desk.

Shonda doing what I did at my U Penn applicant mixer when the stuffy old host said, "I'm not going to give you a lot of *buffalo* about our school . . ." What did I do? What I did was, surrounded by a lot of prep school kids with blond hair and perfect clothes, burst into loud uncontrollable snorting howling laughter. (Needless to say, I did not attend U Penn. Don't smirk. I got in. But I couldn't go there. One of those rich blond kids was gonna see me on campus and tell everyone about the snorting howling laughter.) I do that when I'm nervous. So imagine what it would be like when I'm *extremely* nervous. Live. With Jimmy.

Shonda bursting into loud uncontrollable snorting howling laughter at Jimmy's very first joke, laughter and snorting that gets louder and louder and louder, laughter that I know CANNOT BE STOPPED, that I have no *chance* of stopping despite the absurdity of laughing hysterically in front of Jimmy and Jimmy's live studio audience, a fact which makes me scream with laughter, louder and louder, harder and harder—until the hiccups come.

You can die from the hiccups. For real. I'm a fake doctor

who writes fake medicine for TV. So I know stuff. And I am telling you, we killed Meredith's stepmother with hiccups and that could happen to me. I could laugh until I hiccup and hiccup and die. I could DIE on live TV. Literally die. Do you want me to do that to Jimmy? Do you want me to make Jimmy the guy who killed a guest? I think not.

You know what else you don't want to see?

Shonda having spontaneous fear-snot shoot out of my face.

Fear-snot.

Nuff said.

All of these things could happen if I were to go on live TV. These are all *not* good things. These are bad things. Baaaaaaad things.

You may think I'm exaggerating. Or trying to be funny.

Does fear-snot sound funny to you? Close your eyes and imagine it shooting out of your face in front of twelve million people. It's not funny. It's not funny at all.

Okay, I have never had fear-snot. But I am the kind of person who WOULD GET fear-snot. It would happen to me. Simply because it would be horrifying. That is how the universe likes to treat me, teach me, keep me in line. I'm the girl who splits her pants and does not notice the breeze. I'm the woman who forgets to cut the price tag off my dress and walks around with it stuck to my back so everyone can see not only how much I spent but also WHAT SIZE I AM for an entire dinner party. I'm the one who spills. Who trips. Who drops. I once accidentally flung a chicken bone across the room at a very elegant cocktail party while trying to make a point.

Did you hear me?

I FLUNG A CHICKEN BONE ACROSS THE ROOM AT A COCKTAIL PARTY.

While everyone stared at the chicken bone on the white carpet, I pretended that the culprit was not me. True story.

You can't take me anywhere.

You certainly can't take me somewhere and then film me live in front of millions of people. Because if there is fear-snot to be had, I WILL HAVE IT.

And Chris knows this. He knows what could happen on live TV. He knows how I feel about live TV.

He just doesn't care.

He doesn't have time for fear-snot. He's trying to help me build a career here.

Against my will.

Over the years, every single time that Kimmel's people have asked me to be a guest on *Jimmy Kimmel Live*, I've said no.

And no.

And no.

I don't tell Kimmel's people that I am saying no because live TV is a minefield. I don't tell them that I am saying no because I am afraid I may accidentally Janet Jackson Boob Jimmy. Or pee on his sofa like an excited puppy. Or fall on my face before I even make it to the sofa. Or die. I don't say anything about any of that.

Because I'm a lady, damn it.

I just say no.

Kimmel's people are so nice. When I see them at ABC events, they smile at me while I look at them with my statue face and my swirly eyeballs.

Then I shuffle to the buffet table to put some food on top of my stress.

I am pretty sure that the super-nice Kimmel people think I'm an asshole.

My publicist, Chris, doesn't think I'm an asshole. He thinks I am a pain in the ass. To him, I am the Sisyphean ball he has been shoving up this same hill for years now. And yet he continues to believe. He continues to hope.

He keeps hope *alive*.

He uses buzzwords. Buzzwords we both know I can't just say no to. They want to do an *hour-long* Scandal *special*. On *finale* night. *ABC is excited.* And it's a delicate time for me and ABC right now. So I have to be a team player. If I say no, I am not being a good team player. All that Athlete Talk will have been for nothing.

See, I am in the middle of negotiations for my next contract.

You understand what I'm saying?

Athlete Talk has to MEAN something.

We sit on the phone together. I am silent. I'm hoping he'll get the hint, hang up and call ABC and tell them I have the plague. It could happen. I could get the plague. I feel it coming on right now.

Chris doesn't hang up. He never hangs up.

He's silent.

He's waiting me out. This is a contest we engage in frequently. Finally, as always, I speak first.

"I do not want to be on television. Ever," I remind him. "Never. Ever. For any reason. No one needs to see me. Why would anyone need to see me when they could be seeing Kerry Washington?"

I believe this deeply. Have you seen Kerry Washington? Kerry Washington is extraordinary.

"Kerry Washington just had a baby," Chris reminds me.

Right. Kerry is quite rightly taking some much-needed bonding time with her new baby. Mother to mother, I feel solidarity with her on that. Damn.

"Tony then! Or Bellamy! Bellamy is amazing!"

I start calling out the names of *Scandal* actors. Chris takes a deep breath. Then he lists all the reasons why I should be on TV. These reasons make no sense to me. He may as well be speaking German. Because I don't speak German. Or that really cool Khoisan language in Namibia that is just a series of clicks.

"I do not understand a thing you are saying!" I holler.

"Why would I want to be *more* recognizable? That is the exact opposite of what I want to be!! Make this go away!"

Chris is now likely contemplating whether it will be more satisfying to sew a suit made out of my skin or to simply scatter the chopped-up pieces of my corpse in the ocean.

Maybe he's just thinking about hobbling me, Stephen King *Misery*–style.

I wouldn't blame him. I'd fight him, but I wouldn't blame him. I mean, I am screaming at him. I am actually screaming at him in a hysterical voice. Fear is taking over. I'm losing it. I can *feel* myself losing it and a part of me wants to hobble me too. Because, dude: when you become a person with any kind of power, don't ever become a person who screams. Even in hysterical fear.

The things that you can do when you are at the bottom of the ladder change as you move up. At the top of that ladder, doing many of those very same things makes you an asshole. I'm being an asshole. A very scared, very shy asshole.

Chris is quiet for a long, long, long moment.

He's going to place my head in a box like that guy did to Brad Pitt's girlfriend in *Seven*. I know it. I don't want my head in a box. My head will not look good in a box. I listen nervously to the silence.

But when he speaks, his voice has the calm tone of power and triumph.

He's going to win. And he knows it.

Here's why:

"Shonda," he says, "I thought you were saying yes to everything. Or was that just big talk?"

Damn.

Checkmate.

Maybe I can put *his* head in a box.

yesyesyesyesyesyesyesyesyesyesyesyesyesyesyesyesyes

I thought saying YES would feel good. I thought it would feel freeing. Like Julie Andrews spinning around on that big mountaintop at the beginning of *The Sound of Music*. Like Angela Bassett when she's Tina Turner and she walks out of that divorce court and away from Ike with nothing but her name in *What's Love Got to Do with It*. Like how you feel when you have just finished baking double-fudge brownies but you have yet to shove one into your mouth, starting the sugar rush roller coaster that won't end until you are curled up in a ball on the sofa, rocking back and forth while scraping the crumbs of the empty brownie pan into your mouth and trying to talk yourself into believing that maybe the ex-boyfriend you dumped wasn't so bad after all.

Like that.

This *YES* does not feel like a post-baked, pre-eaten brownie.

I feel forced into this. I feel like I don't have a choice. My obligation to my network plus my obligation to my stupid Year of Yes idea has trapped me.

My paw is caught in a trap. I can try to chew it off and run away. But if you think I am whining now? Try me when I'm down a paw and have just a bloody gnawed stump to deal with.

The tears.

The drama.

The wailing and moaning.

The cross I would be nailing myself to would be so pretty and brightly lit. Oh, my cross wouldn't be missed by anyone! You'd see my cross from space.

The numbing fear is starting to creep over me. This is going to be a terrible experience. It's going to eat me alive. My left eye starts to twitch. I tell myself that it's okay, because it is twitching only in what I am sure is the tiniest, most unnoticeable way. Nobody can tell it is twitching but me.

"Wow, your eye is really twitching," Joan Rater, head writer at *Grey's Anatomy*, informs me with great authority. The whole writing staff crowds around to peer at my eyeball jumping around in my head.

"Honey," my toddler, Emerson, takes my face in her hands and gravely informs me, "your eye is broken. It's busted, honey."

This is not going to be okay.

This is not what *YES* is supposed to feel like.

If it is, this is going to be the longest year of my life.

Later that same week, I'm sitting on the soundstage at *Grey's Anatomy*. Cranky as hell. It is not enough that my eyeball is still twitching merrily away. It's Season Ten. Sandra Oh is leaving the show. As we move closer to her final episode, every scene with her begins to feel more and more special. We are all very aware that a rare talent is soon going to be walking out the door. I've come to set for the rehearsal of a big scene.

To help close out Cristina's story line, Isaiah Washington has returned to do us the honor and favor of scrubbing in as Preston Burke. Right now, in this scene, Preston is telling Cristina that he is giving her his hospital—like Willy Wonka giving away the Chocolate Factory. It's the biggest moment of the show for Cristina, the culmination of ten seasons of character growth. She stands face-to-face with the man she almost destroyed herself loving. She'd once lost herself in his orbit, revolving around him, desperately in need of his sun. She'd made herself smaller to accommodate his greatness. Now she has surpassed him. And he is paying his respects. He has come to praise her. The Chocolate Factory is hers if she wants it.

One half of the Twisted Sisters is getting her fairy-tale ending: she's being offered what she has earned, she's being recognized for her brilliance and she is being rewarded with her dreams come true. It may not be the fairy-tale ending anyone else would want or would want *for* her, but Cristina does not give a damn. Frankly, neither do I. Cristina deserves her joy.

This is what joy looks like to a woman with genius.

And as I watch Sandra Oh's face tell a whole story as she brilliantly gives nuance to the moment Cristina realizes Burke is handing her the keys to the kingdom, I realize why Cristina's journey can end. I realize why it is time to let this character go and be happy for her.

Cristina has learned what she needs to know. Her toolbox is full. She has learned to not let go of the pieces of herself that she needs in order to be what someone else wants. She's learned not to compromise. She's learned not to settle. She's learned, as difficult as it is, how to be her own sun.

If only real life were so simple.

But my eye stops twitching.

And I pick up the phone and I call Chris.

"Janet Jackson Boob," I tell him. "Fear-snot. Chicken bone."

There's a long silence while Chris perhaps worries that I have had a stroke.

"Huh?"

"It can't be live. I will do *Jimmy Kimmel*. But it can't be live," I say firmly.

I can hear Chris breathing in and out. He's going to eat my kidney and liver with a fine wine.

"Let me get this straight," he says tightly. "You will be on *Jimmy Kimmel LIVE*. As long as it is not LIVE."

He says this as if speaking to a crazy person. And maybe he is.

But I just watched Cristina Yang get her Chocolate Factory. I'm feeling bold. I'm not compromising. I don't need to settle.

"Exactly," I tell him.

If I have to be on TV, if I have to do something as scary as *Kimmel*, we're going to do it my way or we don't do it at all.

See, I'm keeping all my pieces.

I don't want brownies.

I want a whole damn Chocolate Factory.

YES should feel like the sun.

yesyesyesyesyesyesyesyesyesyesyesyesyesyesyesyes

I have no idea how it happened or what conversations took place or whose baby he had to steal or what favor I now owe to what stranger or which warlord I am now betrothed to.

I do not know. And I do not care.

Chris did it.

The man made rain.

Which is how, the week before the *Scandal* finale aired, I found myself sitting on the set of Pope & Associates with Jimmy Kimmel filming an hour-long *not*-live special called *Jimmy Kimmel Live: Behind the Scandalabra.*

Jimmy was incredibly nice to me. He told me funny stories and asked me about my children while we waited for the camera to roll. Before every take he patiently told me what was going to happen next and then he told me the very same thing *again*, like he knew I had the brain of a very demented senior citizen who could only remember two or three words at a time. He kept asking me if I was okay. And if he thought it was weird that I became a block of solid wood and could not seem to both walk and talk while the camera was rolling, he kept it to himself. He simply arranged it so I never had to walk and talk at the same time. In fact, he made it so I barely had to talk. I'm serious. Go online. Watch it. What am I doing?

1. Smiling.
2. Trying really hard not to look directly into the camera.
3. Laughing at Jimmy's jokes.
4. Holding a really big glass while Scott Foley pours wine into it.
5. Looking directly into the camera even though I've been told not to A LOT.
6. Laughing at Jimmy's jokes some more.

Jimmy did *all* the work. I didn't have to do anything. And yet. He made it SEEM like I did stuff. Everyone thought I did all kinds of stuff. So he did all the work and I got all the credit.

Like when a baby poops.

Everyone fawns over the baby. Now, who is the one cleaning up the poop? *Not* the baby, I can tell you that. But no one is fawning over the person carrying that smelly diaper to the trash.

I think I just likened myself to a pooping baby. But you get my point. Jimmy did all kinds of amazing things to make me look good. And because Jimmy does his show all the time and is always amazing, everyone just nodded and smiled at him. But because there was a very good chance that there would be fear-snot and chicken bones surrounding me, I got a standing ovation from everyone I know.

I got calls. I got emails. I got tweets and facebooks and all the other social media things people get.

The next day, I also got the biggest delivery of red roses ever.

EVER.

Like "horse winning the Kentucky Derby" big.

They came in a giant silver vase. A vase so huge and heavy that it took three men to carry it into the house. My daughter Harper tried counting the red roses but lost interest after ninety-eight.

The dozens and dozens of red roses were from Jimmy.

He wasn't proposing marriage.

The ratings had come out. *Jimmy Kimmel Live* beat *The*

Tonight Show Starring Jimmy Fallon for the very first time ever with that episode.

That was the nicest thing.

Kimmel beat Fallon. Which meant Kimmel was right to keep asking me to be on the show. And Chris was right to force me to do it. And I guess I was right to ask that it be taped. Because I do not know if the results would have been the same if I'd been unable to come out on live TV because I was having a full-scale meltdown in the corner of the *Jimmy Kimmel Live* dressing room.

But none of that mattered to me. Not really. I mean, I was grateful that Jimmy was happy. I was grateful that I hadn't messed up one of his shows. But overwhelmingly, I could only think about one thing:

I did it.

I said yes to something that terrified me. And then I did it. *And I didn't die.*

There's a crack in the pantry door. A sliver of light coming in. I can feel a bit of warm sun on my face.

I wander over to Chris.

"Thank you," I mumble.

"What? I didn't hear you."

"THANK YOU."

Chris grins. Triumphant.

He heard me the first time. You know he did. I know he did. We ALL know he did. But I don't mind.

Fear-snot. Chicken bone. Adele Dazeem.

What do I care? It *happened*. I did it.

And I kept all my pieces.

YES does feel like the sun.

Maybe I'm building my own damn Chocolate Factory.

5

Yes to Speaking the Whole Truth

Early in 2014, I'm invited to join a small private women's online network. It quickly becomes a lifeline for me. It's full of smart women who do interesting things, and I look forward to its missives. Fascinating conversations fly back and forth all day over email. New to the group, I mind my Ps and Qs and keep my mouth shut. I'm an observer, a listener. I wander on the outskirts. Rarely do I consider even joining the conversation.

On May 29, about a week and a half before I am due to stand at the podium at Dartmouth College and deliver the required twenty-to-thirty-minute commencement address to an audience of what is now a roughly estimated sixteen thousand people, I write the following email to the group:

FROM: Shonda

TO: The Group

RE: My Death

So it's happening soon. My commencement speech. And (shocker!) I haven't written a word. I got totally paralyzed. The paralyzing moment happened when I was brushing my teeth and listening to NPR and heard someone on there (someone I love and admire) say that one of the speeches they were most looking forward to discussing was . . . mine.

No pressure. No pressure at all.

Apparently now, these speeches are filmed and streamed and uploaded and tweeted and dissected and NPR has a WHOLE site dedicated to dissecting them.

People don't faint when they give these speeches, right? That has not happened?

Do you see what I said there?
I said that I have not written a word.
And it is true. Less than two weeks from the day.
I have not written a word.
NOT ONE SINGLE WORD.
I wander around feeling white-hot terror searing all cre-

ativity out of my brain. The fires of failure are whipping around, burning down any ideas I may have had.

It's a writing apocalypse up in my imagination.

I lie on the floor of my office. I drink red wine. I eat popcorn. I hug my kids. I prepare for the end of days.

Every work email I write in those ten days before the speech says basically the same thing: *Why are you asking me whatever thing you are asking me? Don't you know I am about to die of humiliation and fear while giving a speech? Let me have this time to say good-bye to my family!*

I become nonsensical. Irrational. I stop speaking out loud. I make noises instead.

"Grmmph," I say to my assistant, Abby, when she asks me if I would like to take a certain meeting.

"Bllummppth," I mutter to the writers when they ask if I have any story ideas.

The women in my online network send me words of support. They send advice. They remind me to power pose.

"Power pose like Wonder Woman!"

Power posing like Wonder Woman is when you stand up like a badass—legs in a wide stance, chin up, hands on your hips. Like you own the place. Like you have on magical silver bracelets and know how to use them. Like your superhero cape is flapping in the wind behind you.

I'm not just some dork telling you to pretend to be Wonder Woman.

It's a real thing.

My online network tells me to power pose like Wonder Woman and reminds me of the actual studies that say that power posing like Wonder Woman for five minutes not only improves self-esteem but even hours later improves how others perceive you.

Let me say that again.

Standing around like Wonder Woman in the morning can make people think you are more amazing at lunchtime.

Crazy. But true.

How awesome is that?

(You don't believe me? Watch the TED Talk.)

I start power posing every time I step into an elevator. It makes for some awkward rides up and down with strangers. But I soldier on. I'll take whatever help I can get.

More wisdom comes in. One of the women writes with this helpful gem: she wants me to remember that the worst thing that can happen to me is that I'll crap my pants onstage. As long as that doesn't happen, she instructs me, I'll be fine.

Surprisingly, this pants-crapping information somehow makes me feel better. Calmer. Because crapping my pants is not a thing I do. My certainty on this matter makes it possible for me to sleep at night. It also allows me to begin writing bits and pieces of my speech. Which I do on little scraps of paper that I continuously lose. I switch to the Notes app on my phone.

But even as it comes together, I'm not sure the speech is any good. And I don't really have time to think about it. I've just finished producing forty-two episodes of television. It's the fewest number of episodes that I've produced in a long time for any given TV season—but still, I'm bone tired. *Private Practice* took its bow the season before, so I've lost a show. But I've added a child. A CHILD. An actual person, a tiny human. Thankfully, Kerry Washington has added one too and I praise the heavens for the gift of only eighteen episodes of *Scandal* this season. I say it aloud to no one but I'm not sure I could have coped with more. Keeping up with three children, sleeping, working, writing and trying to do it all well has been kicking my ass lately. By that moment in June, I was feeling pretty low about my Mommy Scorecard.

The Mommy Scorecard is a thing I keep in my head. On it is an imaginary series of zeros and tens that get dished out by some imaginary judge-y bitch who looks an awful lot like me. The zeros hit the card when I fail: when I miss a recital because I'm traveling, when I forget that it's my turn to provide food for preschool snack day, when we don't make it to a birthday party because the introvert in me just can't face the magnitude of all the social interaction.

I keep hearing about these Mommy Wars. Debates are raging: which child-rearing style is best, what makes a bad mother, who is to blame for kids with "problems," how involved should you be at the school—it goes on and on. Really, it comes down to this: which kind of mother is screwing up her kid more? People love to talk about these Mommy Wars all the time in magazines. Talk show hosts plead: can't we all come together? But I never really got what everyone was talking about.

The only mommy I am ever at war with is me.

It doesn't help that I now have a tween—a glorious, lanky, stunningly beautiful, future supermodel of a tween—who, like all tweens, possesses a special skill for twisting the knife I've already firmly implanted in my own chest.

"This is the third recital you've missed," she'll remind me. "And . . . are you ever coming to one of my science fairs?"

It's *not* the third recital. And I was just at the science fair last quarter. But she makes it sound like I wasn't. Which makes me feel like I wasn't.

Boom.

A zero.

Now, I'm no fool. I'm not one of those mothers who allows her children to behave like monsters and walk all over me.

I was raised old-school.

I strive to be old-school.

My kids are not my friends. They are my children. My goal is not to get them to like me. My goal is to raise citizens. My world does not revolve around them. The only helicopter in my life is the toy helicopter that the kids play with.

So my response to my daughter Harper isn't a wringing of my hands and a tearful apology. Nobody did any hand-wringing and apologizing while raising me and I turned out . . . a *writer*.

"I work to feed and clothe you. Do you want food and clothes? Then be quiet and show some gratitude."

That is what I say to my tween.

But inside? Zero on the Mommy Scorecard. Knife twisted a little more. And the commencement speech . . . I have less and less time to focus on it, to obsess about it, to worry over it. It's the end of the season, it's the end of the school year.

The day I'm due to fly to Hanover, New Hampshire, I spend the early morning with my youngest daughters. Then I head over to my tween's school to attend the end-of-the-year ceremony. My daughter is receiving an academic award and, while I already know this, she does not. I don't want to miss seeing her face when she finds out. I arrive just in time to see her name called and, as her face lights up, I attack her with my camera for photos. There are hugs, smiles, joy. And though I have reminded her every day for weeks, there is the inevitable disappointed face when she hears me say I need to leave. Knife twisting again, I rush off to the airport.

It's not until I'm on the plane, away from my real life and surrounded by the close friends I've brought with me for support, that I really look at the speech I've written. That I really face it.

For a while, I feel sick. A cold, hard rock settles at the bottom of my stomach. It's the same kind of speech I have always written. Pithy, witty, snappy. It has highs and lows. Jokes. It's smart and shiny. And it sounds just fine. Except I'm not actually saying anything. I'm not revealing anything. I'm not sharing anything. There is nothing of *me* in here. I speak from behind a curtain. It's like a magic trick—I open my mouth but you never actually hear *me*. You just hear my voice. This speech is all Athlete Talk.

I imagine standing up at that podium tomorrow and looking into the faces of those graduates and . . . What? If I say nothing of substance, tell them nothing, share nothing, give nothing . . . why? Why am I even there?

What am I afraid they will see if I am really myself?

I know it's not the graduates. It's the rest of the world. It's all the other people out there who will hear the speech and judge it and criticize it. And know things about me because of it. I don't know if I want them to know me. Because . . . because . . . I still don't truly know me.

What I do know is that I cannot deliver this speech.

I know that I will not deliver this speech.

This speech is not a *YES*.

I read through it four or five more times. Then I tuck it away into a new folder on my laptop. I label the folder CRAP.

And then I start over.

What I write next is less formal, less stuffy, less stylized.

What I write is casual and a little raw and sometimes inappropriate.

But it's honest.

And it sounds like me.

It *is* me.

If I'm going to give a speech, if I'm going to stand up there and give a speech in front of all these people, if I'm going to make this leap . . .

. . . if I'm going to say yes . . .

If I am going to say YES . . .

I might as well say yes to being me.

No Athlete Talk.

No magic tricks.

I just tell the truth.

When I am done, as the plane streaks through the night sky, I hit Save. And I promise myself that I won't think about the speech too much more until I am standing at the podium.

The morning of graduation I am up before dawn. I need to jump up and down. Stretch. Breathe. I spend more than a few moments Power Posing. From the window of my suite at the Hanover Inn, I can see the stage. I can see the traditional Old Pine Lectern that serves as the podium from which I am to speak.

I stare at it for a long time in the sunrise.

I am going to say yes to everything that scares me.

I wait for the wave of fear and panic to wash over me. But it doesn't come. I shrug to myself. It'll be here any minute, I know. I'm tense, waiting for it. Any second, the familiar freezing panic of stage fright will hit me. The tsunami will hit me.

But it never does.

I am nervous. I am scared. But that is all.

The next few hours are a whirlwind. Photos. Gowns and caps. Shaking lots of hands. Waves of nostalgia. And I keep waiting for the attack of nerves that usually renders me useless. That causes me to become a sweaty pile of hyperventilation. I wait as we march to the stage. I wait as I, along with others, am bestowed with my honorary PhD. I'm still waiting when President Hanlon introduces me and shows me the way to the podium.

I step up to the podium.

And then . . .

Something completely special occurs.

If you watch the video, you can see the moment it happens.

I am standing at the podium. I look out at the crowd. I take a deep breath in. I'm still waiting for it—the fear, the panic, the nerves. I'm almost asking for it. Searching for it. Looking around for it. It must be here somewhere. But when I stare out into that crowd of graduating students in their green caps and gowns, all I see is . . . me.

Twenty years ago, I sat in those chairs, in that crowd, in a green cap and gown. Just like them. I recognize them. I know them. That look on their faces. Their eyes filled with uncertainty. And I understand that the fear, the panic, the nerves I am searching for will not come for me today. It has come for them. The fear they are suffering about what lies ahead is far greater than anything I will ever be feeling. And suddenly I am okay. I am no longer afraid to talk to them. I am no longer afraid to stand there alone at the podium for twenty minutes and be honestly, vulnerably myself with them. Because once upon a time, I was them. And sometime in their futures, they will be me.

Whatever I'm going to say is not for me. It isn't for the outside world. It doesn't matter how people react to it or judge it. I'm not talking to anyone but these graduates sitting in front of me. This is just for them.

And so I exhale.

You can see it.

If you watch the video, you can see me exhale.

You can see the very last instant, the very last moment, the very last breath of my fear. From that exhale forth, I am someone new. Someone comfortable. Someone unafraid.

My body relaxes. I smile. I settle into my soul. And for the first time in my life, I stand on a stage and raise my voice to the public with full confidence and not an inch of panic. For the first time in my life, I speak to an audience as myself and I feel joy. Here is what I say:

DARTMOUTH COMMENCEMENT SPEECH

Delivered June 8, 2014

Hanover, New Hampshire

DREAMS ARE FOR LOSERS

President Hanlon, faculty, staff, honored guests, parents, students, families and friends—good morning and congratulations to the Dartmouth graduating class of 2014!

So.

This is weird.

Me giving a speech.

In general, I do not like giving speeches. Giving a speech requires standing in front of large groups of people while they look at you and it also requires talking. I can do the standing part okay. But the "you looking" and the "me talking" . . . I'm NOT a fan. I get this overwhelming feeling of fear.

Terror, really.

Dry mouth, heart beats super fast, everything gets a little bit slow motion.

Like I might pass out. Or die. Or poop my pants or something.

I mean, don't worry. I'm not going to pass out or die or poop my pants. Mainly because just by telling you it could happen, I have somehow neutralized it as an option. Like as if saying it out loud casts some kind of spell where it cannot possibly happen now.

Vomit. I could vomit.

See? Vomiting is now also off the table.

Neutralized it. We're good.

Anyway, the point is, I do not like to give speeches. I'm a writer. I'm a TV writer. I like to write stuff for other people to say. I actually contemplated bringing Ellen Pompeo or Kerry Washington here to say my speech for me . . . but my lawyer pointed out that when you drag someone across state lines against their will, the FBI comes looking for you, so . . .

So I don't like giving speeches. In general. Because of the fear. And the terror. But this speech? This speech, I really did not want to give.

A Dartmouth commencement speech?

Dry mouth. Heart beats so, so fast.

Everything in slow motion.

Pass out, die, poop.

Look, it would be fine if this were, like, twenty years ago. If it was back in the day when I graduated from Dartmouth. Twenty-three years ago, I was sitting right where you are now. And I was listening to Elizabeth Dole speak. And she was great. She was calm, she was confident. It was just . . . different. It felt like she was just talking to a group of people. Like a fireside chat with friends. Just Liddy Dole and nine thousand of her friends. Because it was twenty years ago. And she was JUST talking to a group of people.

Now? Twenty years later? This is no fireside chat. It's not just you and me. This speech is filmed and streamed and tweeted and uploaded. NPR has, like, a whole app dedicated to commencement speeches.

A WHOLE SITE JUST ABOUT COMMENCEMENT SPEECHES.

There are other sites that rate them. And mock them. And dissect them. It's weird. And stressful. And kind of vicious for an introvert perfectionist writer who hates speaking in public in the first place.

When President Hanlon called me—

By the way, I would like to thank President Hanlon for asking me way back in January, thus giving me a full six months of panic and terror to enjoy.

When President Hanlon called me, I almost said no. Almost.

Dry mouth. Heart beats so, so fast. Everything in slow motion. Pass out, die, poop.

But I'm here. I am gonna do it. I'm doing it. You know why?

Because I like a challenge. And because this year I made myself a promise to do the stuff that terrifies me. And because, twenty-plus years ago when I was trudging uphill from the River Cluster through all that snow to get to the Hop for play rehearsal, I never imagined I would one day be HERE. Standing at the Old Pine Lectern. Staring out at all of you. About to throw down on some wisdom for the Dartmouth commencement address. So, you know, moments.

Also, I'm here because I really, really wanted to eat some EBAs.

Okay.

I want to say right now that every single time someone asked me what I was going to talk about in this speech, I would boldly and confidently say that I had all kinds of wisdom to share.

I was lying.

I feel wildly unqualified to be giving advice. There is no wisdom here. So all I can do is talk about some stuff that could maybe be useful to you. From one Dartmouth grad to another. Some stuff that won't ever show up in Meredith Grey voice-overs or Papa Pope monologues. Some stuff I probably shouldn't be telling you here now. Because of the uploading and the streaming and websites. But I am going to pretend that it is twenty years ago. That it is just you and me. That we're having a fireside chat. Screw the outside world and what they think. I've already said the word *poop* like five times already anyway . . . things are getting real up in here.

Wait.

Before I talk to you, I want to talk to your parents. Because the other thing about it being twenty years later is that

I'm a mother now. So I know some things. Some very different things. I have three girls. I've been to the show. You don't know what that means. But your parents do. You think this day is all about you. But your parents . . . the people who raised you . . . the people who endured you . . . they potty-trained you, they taught you to read, they survived you as a teenager, they have suffered twenty-one years and not once did they kill you. This day . . . you call it your graduation day. But this day is not about you. This is their day. This is the day they take back their lives, this is the day they earn their freedom. This day is their independence day. Parents, I salute you. And as I have an eight-month-old, I hope to join your ranks of freedom in twenty years!!

Okay.

So here it comes. The real-deal part of my speech. Or as you may call it, *Stuff Some Random Alum Who Makes TV Shows Thinks You Should Know Before You Graduate*.

You ready? Here we go!

When people give these kinds of speeches, they usually tell you all kinds of wise and heartfelt things. They have wisdom to impart. They have lessons to share. They tell you: Follow your dreams. Listen to your spirit. Change the world. Make your mark. Find your inner voice and make it sing. Embrace failure. Dream. Dream and dream big. As a matter of fact, dream and don't stop dreaming until your dream comes true.

I think that's crap.

I think a lot of people dream. And while they are busy dreaming, the really happy people, the really successful people, the really interesting, powerful, engaged people? Are busy doing.

The dreamers. They stare at the sky and they make plans and they hope and they think and they talk about it endlessly. And they start a lot of sentences with "I want to be . . ." or "I wish . . ."

"I want to be a writer." "I wish I could travel around the world."

And they dream of it. The buttoned-up ones meet for cocktails and they all brag about their dreams. The hippie ones have vision boards and they meditate on their dreams. You write in your journal about your dreams. Or discuss it endlessly with your best friend or your girlfriend or your mother. And it feels really good. You're talking about it. You're planning it. Kind of. You are blue-skying your life. And that is what everyone says you should do. Right? That's what Oprah and Bill Gates did to get successful, right?

NO.

Dreams are lovely. But they are just dreams. Fleeting, ephemeral. Pretty. But dreams do not come true just because you dream them. It's hard work that makes things happen. It's hard work that creates change.

LESSON ONE: DITCH THE DREAM.
BE A DOER, NOT A DREAMER.

Maybe you know exactly what you dream of being. Or maybe you're paralyzed because you have no idea what your passion is. The truth is, it doesn't matter. You don't have to know. You just have to keep moving forward. You just have to keep doing something, seizing the next opportunity, staying open to trying something new. It doesn't have to fit your vision of the perfect job or the perfect life. Perfect is boring, and dreams are not real. Just . . . DO. You think, "I wish I could travel"—you sell your crappy car and buy a ticket and go to Bangkok right now. I'm serious. You say, "I want to be a writer"—guess what? A writer is someone who writes every day. Start writing. Or: You don't have a job? Get one. ANY JOB. Don't sit at home waiting for the magical dream opportunity. Who are you? Prince William? No. Get a job. Work. Do until you can do something else.

I did not dream of being a TV writer. Never, not once when I was here in the hallowed halls of the Ivy League, did I say to myself, "Self, I want to write TV."

You know what I wanted to be?

I wanted to be Nobel Prize–winning author Toni Morrison.

That was my dream. I blue-skyed it like crazy. I dreamed

and dreamed. And while I was dreaming, I was living in my sister's basement. Dreamers often end up living in the basements of relatives, FYI. Anyway, there I was in that basement; I was dreaming of being Nobel Prize–winning author Toni Morrison. Guess what? I couldn't be Nobel Prize–winning author Toni Morrison. Because Toni Morrison already had that job and she wasn't interested in giving it up. One day I was sitting in that basement and I read an article in the *New York Times* that said it was harder to get into USC film school than it was to get into Harvard Law School.

I could dream about being Toni Morrison. Or I could do.

At film school, I discovered an entirely new way of telling stories. A way that suited me. A way that brought me joy. A way that flipped this switch in my brain and changed the way I saw the world.

Years later, I had dinner with Toni Morrison.

All she wanted to talk about was *Grey's Anatomy*.

That never would have happened if I hadn't stopped dreaming of becoming her and gotten busy becoming myself.

LESSON TWO: TOMORROW IS GOING TO BE THE WORST DAY EVER FOR YOU.

When I graduated from Dartmouth that day in 1991, when I was sitting right where you are and I was staring up at Elizabeth Dole speaking, I will admit that I have no idea what she was saying. Couldn't even listen to her. Not because I was overwhelmed or emotional or any of that. But because I had a serious hangover. Like, an epic painful hangover because—

(And here is where I apologize to President Hanlon, because I know you are trying to build a better and more responsible Dartmouth and I applaud you and I admire you and it is VERY necessary . . .)

—I'd been really freaking drunk the night before. And the reason I'd been so drunk the night before, the reason I'd done upside-down margarita shots at Bones Gate, was because I knew that after graduation, I was going to take off my cap and gown, my parents were going to pack my stuff in the car and I was going to go home and probably never come back to Hanover again. And even if I did come back, it wouldn't matter because it wouldn't be the same because I didn't live here anymore.

On my graduation day, I was grieving.

My friends were celebrating. They were partying. So excited. So happy. No more school, no more books, no more teachers' dirty looks, yay. And I was like, are you freaking kidding me? You get all the fro-yo you want here! The gym is free. The apartments in Manhattan are smaller than my suite in North Mass. Who cared if there was no place to get my hair done? All my friends were here. I ran my own theater company here.

I was grieving.

I knew enough about how the world works, about how adulthood plays out, to be grieving.

Here's where I am going to embarrass myself and make you all feel better about yourselves. I literally lay on the floor of my dorm room and cried while my mother packed my room. I refused to help her. Like, refused. Like, hell no I won't go. I nonviolent-protested leaving here. Like, went limp like a protester only without the chanting—it was really pathetic.

Don't you feel better?

If none of you lie facedown on a dirty hardwood floor and cry today while your mommy packs up your dorm room, you are already starting your careers out ahead of me. You are winning.

But here's the thing. The thing I really felt like I knew. The real world sucks. And it is scary.

College is awesome.

You're special here. You're in the Ivy League, you are at the pinnacle of your life's goals at this point—your entire life up until now has been about getting into a great college and then graduating from that college. And now, today, you have done it. Yay!

The moment you get out of college, you think you are going to take the world by storm. All doors will be opened to you. It's going to be laughter and diamonds and soirees left and right.

What really happens is that, to the rest of the world, you are now the bottom of the heap. Maybe an intern. Possibly a low-paid assistant. At best. And it is awful. The real world, it sucked so badly for me. I felt like a loser all the time. And more than a loser? I felt lost.

Which brings me to clarify LESSON NUMBER TWO: *Tomorrow IS going to be the worst day ever for you.*

But don't be an asshole.

Here's the thing. Yes, it is hard out there. But hard? Is relative. I come from a middle-class family, my parents are academics, I was born after the civil rights movement, I was a toddler during the women's movement, I live in the United States of America, all of which means I'm allowed to own my freedom, my rights, my voice and my uterus and I went to Dartmouth and earned an Ivy League degree.

The lint in my navel that accumulated while I gazed at it as I suffered from feeling lost about how hard it was to not feel special after graduation . . . that navel lint was embarrassed for me.

Elsewhere in the world, girls are being harmed simply because they want to get an education. Slavery still exists. Children still die from malnutrition. In this country, we lose more people to handgun violence than any other nation in the world. Sexual assault against women in America is pervasive and disturbing and continues at an alarming rate.

So yes, tomorrow may suck for you—as it did for me. But as you stare at the lint in your navel, have some perspective.

We are incredibly lucky. We have been given a gift. An incredible education has been placed before us. We ate all the fro-yo we could get our hands on. We skied. We had EBAs at one a.m. We built bonfires and got frostbite and enjoyed all the free treadmills. We beer-ponged our asses off.

Now it's time to pay it forward.

Find a cause you love. It's okay to just pick one. You are going to need to spend a lot of time out in the real world trying to figure out how to stop being a lost loser so one cause is good. But find *one*. And devote some time every week to it.

And while we are discussing this, let me say a thing. A hashtag is not helping.

#yesallwomen

#takebackthenight

#notallmen

#bringbackourgirls

#StopPretendingHashtagsAreTheSameAsDoingSomething

Hashtags are very pretty on Twitter. I love them. I will hashtag myself into next week. But a hashtag is not a movement. A hashtag does not make you Dr. King. A hashtag does not change anything. It's a hashtag. It's you, sitting on your butt, typing into your computer and then going back to binge-watching your favorite show. For me, it's *Game of Thrones*.

Volunteer some hours. Focus on something outside your-self. Devote a slice of your energies toward making the world suck less every week. Some people suggest that doing this will increase your sense of well-being. Some say it's just good karma. I say that it will allow you to remember that, whether you are a legacy or the first in your family to go to college, the air you are breathing right now is rare air. Appreciate it. And don't be an asshole.

LESSON THREE

So you're giving back and you're out there doing and it's working. Life is good. You are making it. You're a success. And it's exciting and great. At least it is for me. I love my life. I have three TV shows at work and I have three daughters at home. And it's all amazing. I am truly happy.

And people are constantly asking me, how do you do it?

And usually, they have this sort of admiring and amazed tone.

Shonda, how do you do it all?

Like I'm full of magical magic and wisdom and special-ness.

How do you do it all?

And I usually just smile and say, "I'm really organized." Or if I'm feeling slightly kind, I say, "I have a lot of help."

And those things are true. But they also aren't true.

And this is the thing that I really want to say. To all of you. Not just to the women out there. Although this will matter to you women a great deal as you enter the workforce and try to figure out how to juggle work and family. But it will also matter to the men. Who I think increasingly are also trying to figure out how to juggle work and family. And frankly, if you are not trying to figure it out, men of Dartmouth? You should be. Fatherhood is being redefined at a lightning-fast rate. You don't want to be a dinosaur.

So women AND men of Dartmouth: as you try to figure out the impossible task of juggling work and family and you hear over and over and over again that you just need a lot of help or you just need to be organized or you just need to try just a little bit harder . . . as a very successful woman, a single mother of three, who constantly gets asked the question "How do you do it all?" For once I am going to answer that question with 100 percent honesty here for you now.

Because it's just us.

Because it's our fireside chat.

Because somebody has to tell you the truth.

Shonda, how do you do it all?

The answer is this: I don't.

Whenever you see me somewhere succeeding in one area of my life, that almost certainly means that I am failing in another area of my life.

If I am killing it on a *Scandal* script for work, I'm probably missing bath and story time at home. If I am at home sewing my kids' Halloween costumes, I am probably blowing off a script I was supposed to rewrite. If I'm accepting a prestigious award, I'm missing my baby's first swim lesson. If I am at my daughter's debut in her school musical, I am missing Sandra Oh's last scene ever being filmed at *Grey's Anatomy*.

If I am succeeding at one, I am inevitably failing at the other.

That is the trade-off.

That is the Faustian bargain one makes with the devil that comes with being a powerful working woman who is also a powerful mother. You never feel 100 percent okay, you never get your sea legs, you are always a little nauseous.

Something is always lost.

Something is always missing.

And yet.

I want my daughters to see me and know me as a woman who works. I want that example set for them. I like how proud they are when they come to my offices and know that they come to Shondaland.

There is a land and it is named after their mother.

In their world, mothers run companies. In their world, mothers own Thursday nights. In their world, mothers work. And I am a better mother for it. The woman I am because I get to run Shondaland, because I get to write all day, because I get to spend my days making things up, that woman is a better person—and a better mother. Because that woman is happy. That woman is fulfilled. That woman is whole. I wouldn't want them to know the me that didn't get to do this all day long. I wouldn't want them to know the me who wasn't doing.

SO.

Lesson NUMBER THREE is that ANYONE WHO TELLS YOU THEY ARE DOING IT ALL PERFECTLY IS A LIAR.

Okay.

I fear that I have scared you. Or that I have been bleak. That was not my intention. It is my hope that you run out of here excited, leaning forward, into the wind, ready to take the world by storm. That would be so very fabulous. For you to do what everyone expects of you. For you to just go be exactly the picture of hard-core Dartmouth awesome.

My point, I think, is that it is okay if you don't. My point is that it can be scary to graduate. That you can lie on the hard-wood floor of your dorm room and cry while your mom packs up your stuff. That you can have an impossible dream to be Toni Morrison that you have to let go of. That every day you can feel like you might be failing at work or at your home life. That the real world is hard.

And yet.

You can still wake up every single morning and go, "I have three amazing kids and I have created work that I am proud of and I absolutely love my life and I would not trade it for anyone else's life ever."

You can still wake up one day and find yourself living a life you never even imagined dreaming of.

My dreams did not come true. But I worked really hard. And I ended up building an empire out of my imagination. So my dreams? Can suck it.

You can wake up one day and find that you are interesting and powerful and engaged. You can wake up one day and find that you are a doer.

You can be sitting right where you are now. Looking up at me. Probably—hopefully, I pray for you—hungover. And then twenty years from now, you can wake up and find yourself in the Hanover Inn full of fear and terror because you are going to give the commencement speech.

Dry mouth.

Heart beats so, so fast.

Everything in slow motion.

Pass out, die, poop.

Which one of you will it be? Which member of the class of 2014 will find themselves standing here at the Old Pine Lectern? I checked and it is pretty rare for an alum to speak here. It's pretty much me and Robert Frost and Mr. Rogers.

Which is CRAZY AWESOME.

Which one of you is going to make it up here? I hope it is you. Yes. You. Seriously. You.

No. Seriously. You.

When it happens, you'll know what it feels like.

Dry mouth.

Heart beats so, so fast.

Everything in slow motion.

Graduates, every single one of you, be proud of your accomplishments. Make good on your diplomas.

Remember, you are no longer students. You are no longer works in progress. You are now citizens of the real world. You have a responsibility to become a person worthy of joining and contributing to society.

Who you are today . . . that's who you are.

Be brave.

Be amazing.

Be worthy.

And every single time you get the chance?

Stand up in front of people.

Let them see you. Speak. Be heard.

Go ahead and have the dry mouth.

Let your heart beat so, so fast.

Watch everything move in slow motion.

So what. You what?

You pass out, you die, you poop?

No.

(And this is really the only lesson you'll ever need to know.)

You take it in.

You breathe this rare air.

You feel alive.

You are yourself.

You are truly finally always yourself.

Thank you. Good luck.

6

Yes to Surrendering the Mommy War (Or, Jenny McCarthy Is My Everything)

I have an amazing nanny.

She's wonderful and soulful. She has a sly sense of humor—I've seen her deliver a funnier joke with a single silent raise of her eyebrow than many stand-up comedians. She guards a very sensitive heart—any human suffering brings her to tears. She's smart. Talk down to her and find yourself mentally slapped. She's an excellent judge of character and seems to know an original spirit from a forgery every time. Cross boundaries with her or her charges in any improper way and suffer the wrath of a lion. Get down on your hands and knees with her and the kids, and she will patiently teach and teach until something in you cracks open and you remember who you were as a child and begin to play.

She's principled and firm, rude behavior doesn't materialize in her presence. She's a grown-up who fully sees and knows children as citizens and people and souls. And because she respects children, all children seem to respect her. She is a goddess sent by the universe through the grace of the stars.

Her name is Jenny.

Jenny McCarthy.

I'm not kidding.

She has the same name as a well-known TV personality. A TV personality whose ideas about vaccinations my Jenny McCarthy does not happen to share, she'd want me to tell you.

Jenny McCarthy says vaccinate your kids.

I hired Jenny McCarthy fifteen minutes after I met her. At least, I tried to. She resisted. She had questions. She interviewed *me*. I was nervous. I knew immediately that Jenny McCarthy was a person I wanted in my house, with my family, around my children. I wanted to know her and I wanted to have her know us. As Olivia Pope would say, trust your gut. I trusted my gut. I knew Jenny McCarthy was for us. She has a good heart.

Once, in trying to describe her to someone, I referred to her as a new-wave Mary Poppins, but really, that's not true. She's way more awesome than that Poppins chick. Have you watched that movie as an adult? I mean, really butt-in-the-seat, stare-at-the-screen watched that movie as an adult? Because, if you ask me, Mary Poppins was not a very good nanny. All she had was a bag of endless objects and a kick-ass umbrella. Also I'm pretty sure she was doing drugs and having sex with that chimney sweep.

About two weeks after Jenny began working at the house, she looked at me thoughtfully and said, "You know, I'm your nanny too. Because, Shonda, you need a nanny."

I think maybe I should have been insulted. I mean, she *did* just call me a child. Right? I should have felt some outrage or some affront. Instead, what I felt, overwhelmingly, was relief.

I had been out battling on the front line, doing the best I could against the enemy. But I was battered and bruised. Bombs kept dropping everywhere, I was tiptoeing around land mines left and right. I wanted to go home. I was losing the Mommy War something terrible.

I don't know about you, but the mistakes and missteps I have made since becoming a mother . . . before kids, my confidence could not be dented. Now it's shattered on a daily basis. *I don't know what I am doing.* There is no manual. There's no checklist. There was no one to give lessons. These tiny humans have me caught up, trapped me behind enemy lines. I willingly enlisted, but did I do it for the right reasons? I worry that all I wanted was to look cute in the uniform. Or maybe be in the USO—sing for the troops. Well, I can't sing. But I can play the oboe. Give me a chance and I will play the *hell* out of an oboe for the troops. Instead I am fighting. Front lines. Holding a weapon. I'm not as brave as the others. Not as smart or as strong or as sure that I can make it.

You know the character in the old war movies who always gets shot because he panics and runs?

That character is me as a mother.

I needed help. I needed fresh troops. Or more ammo. Or a medic. Or even just a chaplain for last rites, for the love of . . .

I got Jenny McCarthy.

Jenny McCarthy is the SEAL Team Six of nannies.

I cannot count the number of times some nice reporter has placed a little battered silver recorder in front of my face, flicked it on and, with a kind smile, asked me what I call the Big Questions: *How do I manage work and home? What tips do I have for working moms? What is my secret to finding balance in a busy world?*

I get asked the Big Questions in almost EVERY SINGLE INTERVIEW I do. I hate the Big Questions. I hate being asked the Big Questions ALMOST as much as I hate being asked the Diversity Question—"Why is diversity so important?" (which ranks for me as one of the dumbest questions on the face of the earth, right up there with "Why do people need food and air?" and "Why should women be feminists?").

But as much as I hate the Big Questions, I don't want to be rude to the very nice reporters who ask. I don't think the reporters mean any harm in posing the questions—I think people genuinely wonder. It's just that, before this Year of

Yes, I genuinely didn't know what to say. So I'd find myself smiling at the reporters and giving a lot of different, odd answers.

"Why, Jane, I manage with a lot of organization and a label maker."

"I do laundry *late at night*, Susan."

"Gosh dangit, Bill, I've started meditating on a regular basis!"

Yeah, right. *Late-night laundry* is the cure to getting three kids up and dressed, working a twelve-hour day, making calls to my kid's tutor, scheduling doctor's appointments and play-dates on my only ten-minute break and then coming home to find that my one-year-old finally walked and *I missed it*?

Late-night laundry, my ass.

Late-night laundry is not a true answer to any question ever.

There is one answer to all of those reporters' Big Questions.

I just didn't want to say it.

Because no one else ever said it.

I've read a lot of books written by and about working women and I'm struck by the fact no one ever seems to want to talk about having help at home. Which I think is not so helpful to the women who *don't* have help at home.

Let me put this in completely irrelevant and strange hair-related terms:

God bless the soul of Whitney Houston, but I spent an hour every single morning of all four years of high school in front of the mirror trying to get my hair to look exactly like Whitney's hair. Hours and hours of my life given over to a hot curling iron and a bottle of hair spray and burned fingertips. To me, Whitney's hair was the definition of flawless. As a teenager in Coke-bottle-thick glasses who barely spoke at school and spent all her time inside books, nothing about my life was flawless. I somehow believed that everything would be better if I could just make my hair look like Whitney's. If my hair was flawless, my life would follow suit. Because clearly Whitney had it all worked out.

I was at a hair salon in Los Angeles five or six years after graduating from college. For some reason, Whitney came up in the usual hair salon gossip. I casually mentioned to my hairdresser how much I'd loved her hairstyle when I was in high school and then spun the story of my morning Whitney ritual. I made sure that I danced around the sad determination and kept the story funny. Gotta lay that track, gotta burn that campfire. So my hairdresser was still wiping the tears of laughter from her face when she said it.

"Girl"—she shook her head—"you know that was a wig she had on, right? You could probably buy it if you want to. Hold on. Let me get the wig catalogue and show you . . ."

I did not hear another word she said. I was lost, thinking of the hours of wasted time and the gallons of wasted hair spray. I relived the inevitable misery, the feeling of failure and insecurity that came every morning when my hair wouldn't do what I was trying to bully it into doing.

And if I had known . . . if I had just been told . . . no matter how hard I worked, my hair was NEVER going to look like that . . .

If I had only known that not even *Whitney's* hair could look like that . . .

I had to bite my lip hard to keep from bursting into tears right then and there in front of two ladies I didn't know.

Black hair salons are no joke—I was going to be sitting across from these two ladies for at least five more hours. I did not want to be known as the Fool Who Sobbed While She Got Her Hair Relaxed.

I didn't cry. But it hurt. The betrayal ran deep.

But, I have to admit, there was also a small sense of relief.

Because now I knew: I had not failed.

I just didn't *own the wig*.

Successful, powerful working mothers who keep silent about how they take care of their homes and families, who behave as if they maybe have a clone of themselves or possess Hermione Granger's Time-Turner so they can be two places at once . . . well, they are making everyone else get out their curling irons.

Don't do that. Don't make me get my curling iron out for no reason.

Jenny McCarthy is my family's nanny. And I am proud to say so out loud to anyone who asks. I am proud to say that I do not do this alone.

I don't think powerful, famous women hide the fact that they have nannies or some kind of help at home because they are being unkind to other people. I mean, these women aren't at home laughing and laughing at how everyone out in America is trying to do it all and can't because they don't know that the secret is that NO ONE CAN DO IT ALL! HA HA!! We fooled you! SUCKA!

I don't even think that's why my idol didn't tell us she wore the wig.

Powerful famous women don't say out loud that they have help at home, that they have nannies, housekeepers, chefs, assistants, stylists—whatever it is they have to keep their worlds spinning—they don't say out loud that they have these people at home doing these jobs because they are ashamed.

Or maybe a more precise way to say it is that these women have *been shamed*.

Before my daughter Harper was born, when I was still filling out stacks and stacks of adoption paperwork, smiling for social workers and obsessing over baby clothes in stores— back when having a baby was more one of my brilliant ideas than anything else—a working friend asked me if I had started interviewing.

"Interviewing for what?" I remember asking her.

"You know. A baby nurse, a nanny." She had a new baby herself, a little boy less than six months old. I can still picture her as she said this. She leaned forward in her chair, more intense than I thought the discussion merited. As if she was trying to tell me something important. And of course she was. She *so* was.

She was wasting her time.

I am never more sure of myself about a topic than when I have absolutely no experience with it. So with no baby of my own anywhere in sight, I was incredibly sure of myself as a mother.

If I could slap myself, just reach back in time and wallop a good one across my face . . .

Because what I did next . . .

Look, it didn't feel like much at the time. In my defense, I wasn't yet a mother. I didn't yet know. I'm innocent!

Ignorance is no excuse.

What I did next was cruel. And from where I stand now, after thirteen years fighting deep behind the enemy lines of the Mother Hood, I can tell you with certainty: any tribunal would call it a war crime. What I did next was launch a violent emotional ambush that left my unarmed sister wounded in the field.

I looked at my friend. She had dark circles of exhaustion under her eyes. I'm pretty sure her hair hadn't been washed in weeks. She'd blown her nose with baby wipes earlier. I took all of this in. And I said:

"Why in the world would I *hire* someone to take care of my baby? I mean, seriously? That's just lazy. If I'm not willing to take care of my baby myself, why am I even *having* a baby in the first place?"

I felt all the mighty righteousness in the world.

Her face tightened. The air between us changed. I felt startled by her rage.

Mom down, mom down.

I can't tell you exactly how that meal ended, what was said. But I can tell you that she did not speak to me again.

Ever.

It wasn't until later that I got it. I had an eight-week-old Harper strapped to my chest in a Snugli. I was sweaty; my hair, which had been a cute Afro puff a week or so ago, was now not merely dirty—it was a matted, terrifying Afro-mess that was going to be both painful and time-consuming to try to restore. The pajamas I wore had a stiff, hard patch of dried formula on the front. That stiff, hard patch acted as a fine bug repellant, because it stank like nothing I'd ever smelled before. I was seated in front of my computer, alternately sobbing from an exhaustion so total that I felt sure I could SEE the air moving in blue waves around the room, and trying to write dialogue for the movie I was supposed to have turned in a month ago.

That was how stupid I was. I adopted a baby and still agreed to turn in a script for a movie a *month* later.

If you have no children, trust me: THAT IS BEYOND STUPID.

Later that evening, Christopher arrived. This is Chris #2 for those of you keeping score—not my publicist, Chris. This Chris and I used to be roommates a hundred years ago when we were both broke and struggling. Now he's a lawyer with a wife and an adorable son. I was best man at his wedding. He is Harper's godfather, and he takes that job very seriously. Every Sunday for the past twelve years, he has showed up at my door to spend time with his godchild. Every. Single. Sunday. He got married on a Saturday, and the next day he was at my house. I told him to go home. He told me it was Sunday in a tone that allowed no argument. He's not just a friend—he's family.

So when Chris #2 arrived that evening, he took one look at me and removed the baby from my arms. He gave me that smile you give a person who has the crazy, swirly eyes. He also took a big step back at the smell of me.

"Go take a shower. Harper and I are going to watch ESPN."

When I woke up an hour later I was still in the shower, the now cold water causing me to shiver. I thought: "I need help. I need to hire some help. I need to hire a lot of help. Or I am going to lose my job and my child and I are going to starve to death. I need to hire help or I won't make it."

And I suddenly thought of my friend.

I thought of what I had said to her.

Mom down, mom down.

I thought of what I had done to her.

I'd shamed her.

We've all been taught to shame and be ashamed. And why wouldn't we feel ashamed? How could we not feel ashamed?

We're not supposed to have any help. We're supposed to do it all ourselves. Even if we are working. So if you have kids and you get help to care for them?

SHAME ON YOU.

Which is just . . . rude.

And sexist.

Caterina Scorsone (who also happens to play Amelia Shepherd on *Grey's Anatomy* and *Private Practice*) and I spend a lot of time ranting to each other about this issue.

"No man," she points out often, "has *ever* had to apologize for having help in order to take care of his home and his kids. *Ever*. Why do we?"

She has a point. *Why do we?*

I mean, let's all remember that for *most* women, staying home is not an option. Most women have to work. The majority of women, unless they are wealthy or financially cared for by someone else, have to work. Historically, women have always had to work. Women worked in the fields. Women

were maids. Women raised other women's children. Women
were nurses. Women worked in factories. Women were secretaries. Seamstresses. Telephone operators.

What was different in the past was that people lived closer
to their families. Your mother watched your children. Your
aunt watched them. Your sister. Your cousin Sue. For some
people, this remains true. For most people . . . you need help.
And the crisis of child care in this country is brutal. And
scary. And expensive. It's a lot to handle. I'm betting you
are having a hard time doing it all, feeling good about it and
making it all work.

So it would not help anyone to pick up this book and read
that I merrily tuck a giggling toddler under each arm with
effortless ease and skip to my office, where I run two shows
and produce two more while developing others as I laugh
and laugh and sip champagne with celebrities while we all
eat mounds of food and never gain a pound . . .

It never *ever* helps to think that Whitney's hairdo is *real*.

Leave no mom behind, soldiers. And even *with* help . . .
I'm still in the trenches. Nobody has this thing figured out.

Except doesn't it *feel* like everyone else has figured it out?

I don't know about you, but it's the idea that I'm not mea-
suring up that gets me. I'm constantly worrying and wondering and feeling like I am failing because everywhere I
look, everyone else seems to be thriving. The women around
me are smiling and their kids are smiling and their houses

seem clean and it all looks so great on Pinterest and Instagram and Facebook . . .

I am not an "everything looks great" mom. I am a "barely
hanging on" mom.

I am a hot-mess mama.

I have worn pajamas in the carpool line.

Dirty pajamas.

A long long looooong time ago, at one of the schools my
daughter thankfully no longer attends, I was sitting in that
back-to-school meeting that all schools have at the end of
summer. After the principal gave a warm and rousing welcome, she invited the head of the PTA to the stage. Now, the
head of the PTA was a school parent. A mom. A mom just like
any other mom. If any other mom was tall, gorgeous, whip-
smart and—I gotta say it—practically perfect in every way.

Perfect PTA Mom very cheerfully began to tell us about
the rules for the Friday bake sale rotation schedule that we
were all expected to take part in. (Now, why we were filling
our kids up with sugary baked goods and why we were *selling*
them these baked goods in an effort to raise money when the
tuition at this school already made me involuntarily shudder
every time I thought about it . . . was all beyond me. But
there was a weekly bake sale and we all had to join in. For
Perfect PTA Mom told us so.)

"Finally," this PTA mom finished up, "just so we don't
have any problems like last year, I just want to be clear: all of

the baked goods must be homemade, something you make with your child. That's so much nicer."

Now, maybe it's the Midwesterner in me.

Or the common sense in me.

Or the hot-mess mama in me.

It was something.

Before I even knew it was happening, my mouth had opened and I was speaking in a voice that carried loud and clear across the auditorium.

"Are you *fucking* kidding me?!"

Really loud. LOUD. LOOOOUUD.

Heads whipped around in my direction. Try being *that* mom at your kid's school. I didn't even know I had that in me. But I did. I was mad. I was insulted.

I have a time-consuming job. A job that I love. A job that I love and that I wouldn't trade for the world. But being a writer invades my brain twenty-four hours a day. I dream about the shows. The job takes from me in ways I never expected. And yet I am devoted to it. To the rush, to the track laying, to the *work*.

I *work*. I have a job.

People with jobs often do not have time to bake.

"But being a mother is *also* a job, Shonda."

I can hear someone reading this book saying those words right now.

You know what I say to that?

NO.

IT IS NOT.

Being a mother is not a job.

Stop throwing things at me.

I'm sorry but it is not.

I find it offensive to motherhood to call being a mother a job.

Being a mother *isn't* a job.

It's who someone is.

It's who I am.

You can quit a job. I can't quit being a mother. I'm a mother forever. Mothers are never off the clock, mothers are never on vacation. Being a mother redefines us, reinvents us, destroys and rebuilds us. Being a mother brings us face-to-face with ourselves as children, with our mothers as human beings, with our darkest fears of who we really are. Being a mother requires us to get it together or risk messing up another person forever. Being a mother yanks our hearts out of our bodies and attaches them to our tiny humans and sends them out into the world, forever hostages.

If all of that happened at work, I'd have quit fifty times already. Because there isn't enough money in the world. And my job does not pay me in the smell of baby head and the soft weight of snuggly sleepy toddler on my shoulder. Being a mother is incredibly important. To the naysayers, I growl, do not *diminish* it by calling it a job.

And please, don't ever try to tell me it's the most important job I'll ever have as a way of trying to convince me to stay at home with my children all day.

Don't.

I might punch you in the nose.

The most important job to a woman who has rent, has a car note, has utility bills and needs groceries is one that pays her money to keep her family alive.

Let's stop trying to make ourselves indulge in the crappy mythological lady-cult that makes being a mother seem like work.

Staying at home with your children is an incredible choice to make. And it's awesome and admirable if you make it. Go you.

Being a mother still happens if you don't stay home with your kids. It still happens if you get a job and go to work. It happens if you are an Army Ranger and you're deployed overseas and your kid is staying with your parents.

Still a mother.

Still not a job.

Working or staying home, one is still a mother.

One is not better than the other. Both choices are worthy of the same amount of respect.

Motherhood remains equally, painfully death defying and difficult either way.

It does, it does.

Let's all put down our weapons for a minute, okay?

Perhaps you think that it is important to your child's personal growth to bake goods in your house. More power to you, my sister. I will defend your right to bake your brownies, I will march for your right to home-bake whatever you damn well want to home-bake. But I will take off my earrings and ask someone to hold my purse for the verbal beatdown we will need to engage in if you try to tell me that I must define *my motherhood* in the same terms as yours.

There's room enough for everybody here.

This is a big, big maternity tent.

If I want to buy my brownies from Costco and drop them off in a wrinkled brown paper bag still wrapped in the plastic and foil container with the orange price sticker still attached, guess what?

That's how it's gonna go down.

Suck it, judgies.

I am not telling you to do it that way. You go bake your *ass* off. But we all have to acknowledge that our way is not *the* way.

Did I judge your perfectly made, piping-hot, double-fudge chocolate cupcakes with the hand-whipped frosting? Did I judge the beautiful monogrammed cupcake holder with the coordinating starched apron you have on?

No, I did not.

Because you are my sister.

Also, because I am going to eat of all your cupcakes.

Look, I am devoted to my children. Deeply. But my devotion has nothing to do with home-baked goods. It has nothing to do with making any kind of public show of maternal fabulousness. Because—you know me by now—public displays of any kind of fabulousness are never going to happen for me. I am devoted to knowing my children, to reading books with them, to hearing the stories they tell me and to the conversations we have. To making them citizens of the world. To raising strong feminist human beings who love and believe in themselves. That is hard enough for me without delivering home-baked goods to school on a Friday.

I'm never going to braid anyone's pigtails perfectly. No one's clothes are ever going to be ironed. Clean, yes. Ironed? Not by me. We will never make special crafts for every holiday and then take photos of them to put on Pinterest and Facebook.

Ever.

Never ever.

I will always be resentful of mom activities that take place on a Tuesday at eleven a.m. As if the mothers with jobs are not valued or welcome.

And I am always going to yell "What the fuck!" at the PTA meeting if you tell me the brownies need to be home-made.

I am already in the middle of a Great Mommy War and

it is against my worst enemy—me. I don't need another war against you. I'm betting you don't need one either.

Stacy McKee (who is one of the new head writers at *Grey's Anatomy* but started out way back in the beginning as the assistant on the show) IS the kind of mom who does crafts with her kids and puts photos of them up on Pinterest and Instagram. She works long, hard hours but still, you go into her office and as she's talking scripts and story, she's hot-gluing beads onto a princess cape for her daughter. I always furrow my brow and ask her why the hell she is doing this. Why? Or why the hell is she delicately hand-painting vistas onto Easter eggs? Or why is she doing any number of crazy amazing crafty things Stacy does for her kids? For the love of wine, why?

Stacy will furrow her brow back at me, equally confused.

"Why wouldn't I?" she says.

See, Stacy LOVES doing this stuff. She'd probably do it even if she didn't have kids. Oh wait. I knew her back when she didn't have kids and she WAS doing it. Stacy once spent days making incredibly lifelike renderings of all the *Grey's Anatomy* characters out of pipe cleaners.

PIPE CLEANERS.

So it's not about working moms vs. nonworking moms. It's about people who love hot-gluing beads on capes vs. people who do not know what a hot-glue gun *is*.

And it's not even that.

It's about the non–glue gun people not assuming the glue gun people are judging them, and vice versa. Maybe don't start out with your weapons raised. Maybe that Perfect PTA Mom didn't even realize that homemade brownies could be a hardship. Maybe instead of yelling obscenities at the mention of homemade brownies, it would be better to stand up and gently point out that not everyone has the time or the bandwidth to make brownies.

And if you are met with condescension, *then* yell the obscenities.

This year, at Emerson's new preschool, I was in charge of the cake for the end-of-the-year party. I got lucky and found a bakery that can reproduce photos on a cake. I don't know how they do it and I don't care. I ordered from the bakery and showed up at the party with my awesome store-bought cake. Every child's face smiling out of the frosting. Everyone oohed and aahed. I felt victorious. In a sick, competitive, not-allowed-to-play-Scrabble, kicked-off-of-team-sports maternal fabulousness kind of way. And then someone asked me where the cake cutter was.

I brought the cake.

I did not bring anything with which to cut the cake. Or plates on which to eat the cake. Or any utensils.

At the other school, this might have been an international incident for me. Things might have escalated to nuclear levels. Arsenals would have been emptied.

But now, at this school?

I said, "Um, the cake is sooo pretty."

And I got a laugh. A friendly laugh.

Then someone grinned and said, "No big deal. I have some cake-cutting stuff!"

And everyone just moved on. Cake was served. Cake was consumed. Everyone copied down the name of the bakery off the side of the box. That was that.

These moms leave no mom behind.

I love it here.

I don't think they are different from the moms at the other school. It is that I am different. All the moms were great all along. I just couldn't see it. Now, I'm no longer looking for the enemy. So I no longer see the enemy.

And so finally, in this year, I allow myself to fully lay down my weapons.

When a reporter flicks on that recorder, smiles and asks the Big Questions, I do not call in the troops. I do not raise my shields.

I allow myself to be seen.

"How do you manage work and home? What tips do you have for working moms? What *is* your secret to finding balance in a busy world?"

Yes, I can answer now.

No hot-glue gun.

No home-baked goods.

No late-night laundry.

Leave no mom behind.

"Jenny McCarthy. To do it all, I have Jenny McCarthy."

I feel really good.

Of course, the reporter walks away deeply confused as to why Jenny McCarthy seems to figure so prominently in my life.

But I don't care.

I wave the white flag.

There is victory in surrender.

Curling irons down, my sisters.

The Mommy War has ended.

7

Yes to All Play and No Work

As the Year of Yes began to really go forward, something happened.

I got busier.

And busier.

And busier.

The more I said yes to things that challenged me, the more I had to leave the house. Saying yes had turned little cocooned me into a big social butterfly.

I flew to New York to see Kerry Washington guest-host *Saturday Night Live*. I went to the private parties of incredibly interesting people. I threw a fund-raiser for the Democratic National Committee. I helped host charity events. There were a lot of awards that year because now there was not only one show starring a black woman on Thursday night—there were two. And all three shows on Thursday were from Shondaland. My publicist, Chris, was smartly taking advantage of the fact that I was saying yes and booking as many interviews as he could squeeze into my schedule. I did my first *Good Morning America* interview with Robin Roberts. I went with the cast of *Scandal* to *The View*. I was photographed by Annie Leibovitz. I did a live interview in front of an audience at the Smithsonian. I felt like I was everywhere.

And I was. Everywhere, it seemed, but at home.

Which makes sense. All the things that would challenge me happened outside my home. Inside my home? Doing just fine.

At least I thought I was.

I mean, I was still a hot-mess mama. I was still working too much. I still needed Jenny McCarthy to nanny both the kids and me. I still needed help. I still wasn't getting enough sleep.

But I really thought I was doing fine.

Except I started to feel . . . irrelevant.

In my own home.

I'd come home and Emerson and Beckett would glance my way, give me a nod and then continue playing. Like I was the nice neighbor lady visiting from next door. Or Harper would eye me with disdain when I asked her which friend she was talking about and I'd realize I had missed a whole week's worth of discussions—a lifetime in tween years.

And then I hit an emotional wall.

One night I was all dressed up in a ball gown, hair and makeup done perfectly, borrowed diamonds shimmering on my neck and wrists. Ready to head out to some event that I had said *yes* to. And as I walked through the foyer to the front door, my daughter Emerson came rushing toward me.

"MAMA!!" she was hollering, sticky hands outstretched. "Wanna play?"

For a split second, it felt like time froze. Like in one of those action movies where everything goes into slow motion, then spins around—just before the hero dude (because somehow in the time-freezing, slow-mo, spin-around movies it is ALWAYS a dude) kicks someone's ass. But there's Emerson, her one curly tuft of hair bound into a valiant attempt at a ponytail on the top of her head in a way that makes her look like Tweety Bird. She's frozen, then moving toward me in slow motion, and then the whole room is spinning around and I can see myself: the blue ball gown, the sticky hands, the child hurtling through space toward me.

She's asked me a question.

"Wanna play?"

I'm late. I'm perfectly, elegantly dressed. Carolina Herrera made this gown. The shoes I'm wearing are some kind of navy lace that I find extremely painful, but damn, they look good on me. When I step out onto the stage, the speech I've written for this particular evening in tribute to a friend is funny and vibrant and moving. I know it will be a special moment, something the town will probably talk about the next day. My phone keeps buzzing repeatedly. It's Chris, my publicist. I really should be arriving just about now. But . . .

"Wanna play?"

There's that round face. Big hopeful eyes. She's got cupid-red lips.

I could bend down, grab her hands in mine before she touches me. Give her a soft kiss and tell her, "No. No, Mama has to go, Mama can't be late."

I could.

I'd be well within my rights. It wouldn't be unheard-of. It would be okay. She'd understand.

But in this frozen moment, I'm realizing something.

She didn't call me "*Honey*."

She's not calling everyone "*Honey*" anymore.

She's changing. Right before my eyes. The baby who was on my hip that last Thanksgiving is going to be three years old on her next birthday.

I'm missing it.

And if I'm not careful, she's going to see the back of my head heading out the door more than she'll see my face.

So in that split second, everything changes.

I kick off my painful high heels. I drop to my knees on the hardwood floor, making the ball gown pouf up around my waist like some kind of navy confection. It's going to wrinkle. I don't care.

"Wanna play?" she's asked.

"YES," I say. "Yes, I do."

And I grab those sticky hands in mine and Emerson plops herself down into my lap, laughing as the gown flies up around her.

When I arrive at the venue, fifteen minutes late, the navy ball gown is hopelessly wrinkled and I'm carrying my heels in my hand. But I don't care—there's a hot pearl of joy in my chest that is warming me in a way I'd forgotten was possible. That little fire inside of me has been reignited. Like magic.

Let's not get carried away.

It's just love. That's all it is.

We played. Emerson and I. And we were joined by Beckett and then later Harper. There was a lot of laughing. I gave my best reading of the finest book ever written—*Everyone Poops*. There may have been some dancing and singing to a made-up funky disco version of "Head, Shoulders, Knees and Toes."

There were sticky kisses. Beckett jammed her finger into my nose out of curiosity. Emerson put her head against my chest and listened until she heard my heart. Then she looked at me solemnly. "You are still alive."

Yes, I am.

Days like this, I am still alive.

We finished with our daily performance of that damned gorgeous song Idina Menzel sings in *Frozen* that has some sort of Pied Piper magical hold on all children. Then I got in the car to go to the event. Happy. That warm joy in me. Feeling fundamentally changed. Like I knew a secret that very few people get to learn.

But really, it was just love. That's no secret.

It's just something we forget.

We could all use a little more love.

A lot more love.

I am not a naturally optimistic person. I'm too in my own head to be a constant source of cheer. I have to work at happy. Dark and twisty is where my brain likes to settle. So I can use some reminders of what is good and optimistic and glass-half-full about this world. And nothing does that for me like the faces and souls of my tiny humans.

yesyesyesyesyesyesyesyesyesyesyesyesyesyesyesyes

That night, I come home and engage in what I call the Hollywood Single Mom part of my evening, which involves my forcing the nearest awake human over four feet tall to free me from whatever dress and undergarment contraptions my glam team trapped me in hours before. There have been times in New York where the task has fallen upon a very nice hotel maid. A couple of times, actors from my shows have saved me. Once in Martha's Vineyard, I was forced to ask the very proper older gentleman who was my driver for the afternoon.

(Are you judging? I see that look on your face. Uh-uh.

What did I say at the beginning of this book? Well, you are definitely *not* gonna come up here all the way in the middle of this book and judge me. It was either ask or spend the entire night sleeping in a white cocktail dress.)

This time, thankfully, I can ask my babysitter. There's a corset involved, and as soon as there's air flowing back into all parts of my lungs, I pull on a robe and go stick my face around doorways to peek at my sleeping kids.

Staring at each of my girls, I make a decision.

Whenever Emerson or Beckett or Harper (in her own way) asks, "Wanna play?"

I am always going to answer: *YES.*

Always.

Because if I have to have a dress removed by a stranger, I should at least get to do something I enjoy. I should at least get to see that happy look on their faces.

Get a little more love.

And so that's what I do.

I actually do it.

Wanna play?

From now on, the answer is always yes.

I drop whatever I am doing and I go to my children and I play.

It's a rule. No. I've made it more than a rule. I've made it law. Canon. Text. It's a religion. There's a strict obedience to it. Something that I practice. With fervor.

Imperfectly.

But faithfully.

Unquestioningly.

Making it such a steadfast rule allows me to peel away some of the work pressure I put on myself. To know that I "don't have a choice" means that I don't feel any guilt stepping away from my workaholic tendencies. I feel no remorse dumping my purse and coat on the floor just as I'm walking out the door to head to the office when I hear those two magic words—*wanna play*? Those two words have me out of my shoes and sitting at the tiny pink tea table coloring a bunny or playing with the unfortunate one-eyed baby doll or staring at lizards in the garden in an instant.

It's hard to nail down a tween—if you have one, you know what I mean. I vividly remember being twelve years old. I sometimes wonder how my parents allowed me to survive. At that age, the existence of one's parents is nothing more than an embarrassment. Clearly a twelve-year-old is never going to say "Wanna play?" But with Harper, I've learned to look for the words and signs that mean the same thing. If she wanders into my room in the evening and lies down on any piece of my furniture, I put down what I'm working on and give her my full attention. Sometimes that pays off. Sometimes it doesn't. But what I've come to understand is that letting her know my full attention is available is more important than anything else.

Also? I have discovered something about this tall, gangly

girl I love so much that sometimes she has to say "Please stop hugging me" so I will stop: I really *like* her.

She's *interesting*.

I'm discovering her. She's like an endless mystery. I can't wait to see how she's going to turn out.

It may be different for you. Your happy place. Your joy. The place where life feels more good than not good. It doesn't have to be kids. My producing partner Betsy Beers would tell me that for her that place is her dog. My friend Scott would probably tell me that for him it is spending time being creative. You might say it's being with your best friend. Your boyfriend, your girlfriend. A parent. A sibling. It's different for everyone. For some of you, it might even be work. And that, too, is valid.

This *Yes* is about giving yourself the permission to shift the focus of what is a priority from what's good for you over to what makes you feel good.

(Wait. Not heroin. Heroin is not your happy place.

Just cross all drugs off the list.

Are we clear? Okay.

Find a good happy place. A positive one.)

I have shifted my priorities. My job is still incredibly important. It's just that playing with my kids is now *more* important than my job.

In case the idea of doing this makes you nervous, makes you anxious, freaks you out? Makes you think I'm an idiot?

You might say, "That's all very nice for you, Shonda.

You're the boss at your job but I am a cashier so please tell me how I can turn my back on my job and still feed my family, stupid TV lady with your lace shoes and your diamonds. I hope your tiara squeezes your brains right out of your head."

I agree with you.

Whitney Houston. Curling iron. Solidarity.

But here's the thing that I hope helps. Here's the thing that I learned very quickly: nobody wants to spend that much time with me. Or with you. You know why?

You aren't Taylor Swift.

Or Curious George.

Or Rihanna.

Or the Muppets.

I mean that in a good way. A great way.

I mean that you can do this. I mean no matter how busy you are, how hectic your life is, you can probably pull this off in some way.

Emerson and Beckett only ever want to play with me for fifteen minutes or so before they lose interest and want to go do something else. It's an amazing fifteen minutes. But it's fifteen minutes. After fifteen minutes, I'm no one. If I'm not a grasshopper in the yard or a Popsicle or the Very Hungry Caterpillar, I may as well be a tree. Most of the time, Harper only ever wants to talk to me for fifteen minutes as well—sometimes less. I can pull off fifteen minutes . . . I can

TOTALLY pull off fifteen minutes of uninterrupted time even on my worst day.

Uninterrupted is the key: no cell phone, no laundry, no dinner, no anything. You have a busy life. You have to get dinner on the table. You have to make sure they get homework done. You have to force them to bathe. But you can do fifteen minutes.

While I was shocked to discover how little time this Yes to Play commitment really took and how easy it was to incorporate it into my daily life, it was about more than this. What was most difficult was what it forced me to face about myself.

I discovered that age-old cliché is true: people do what they like to do. I work because I like working—I am good at it, it works for me, it's my comfort zone. Knowing, facing the fact that I was more comfortable on a soundstage than on a swing set was incredibly difficult to *handle*. What kind of person is more comfortable working than relaxing? Well . . . me. So this Yes required me to change. It's a difficult challenge for a hard-working, straight-A, obsessive perfectionist to leap into a lifestyle practice that requires dropping everything to . . . *play*.

As I've said, my earliest memories were of imagining in the pantry. As I got older, I preferred the library to any other play space, the books inside to any other companion. When forced outdoors for fresh air and sunshine, I grabbed a book and stuffed it down the back of my pants to hide my contraband. Then I'd climb the willow tree in our backyard and read until my mother allowed me back in. Playing . . . ? I don't remember any real playing . . .

My nanny, Jenny McCarthy, watches all this unfold with solemn eyes. She watches me drop my bags and get down on the floor, awkward and stiff. She offers suggestions.

"You should play with the blocks."

"What if you all did some painting?"

Jenny McCarthy is quietly guiding me. Teaching me how to play. Teaching the stiff, introverted workaholic in me what play means for those outside the pantry doors, outside the library shelves. She's teaching me how to reach and connect with these little extroverts so different from me.

I feel like some kind of alien. Never before on this planet. Learning what this world is like. Jenny McCarthy is showing me how to live. Through these tiny karmic beings sent by the universe to help roll the rock away from the door of my cave and shove me into that bright beautiful sun.

And I am grateful.

We run around the yard. Up and back and up and back. We have thirty-second dance parties in the kitchen. We sing show tunes. We play with baby dolls and hand puppets and Fisher-Price farms.

It's the bubbles that do it.

I'm sitting in the backyard blowing an endless series of bubbles for the girls. The bubbles are filling the air; I'm on a roll, blowing as fast as I can to create a sea of bubbles all around their faces. They are squealing, popping bubbles and tasting bubbles and chasing bubbles. Beckett runs over and presses her sweaty body into me. She has that slight musky dirty kid smell. It always smells to me like . . .

"You smell like puppies!" I tell them.

And suddenly a painting is hung back on my wall:

My mother's in the backyard tending to her big round roses. The sun has just gone down. And my sister Sandie and I are racing around the backyard, each with a glass Mason jar. Trying to catch fireflies. Squealing and chasing fireflies, catching them, staring at them, our faces glowing in their light. Then, just when my mother calls for bedtime, we open the jars and release them into the night air.

"You smell like puppies," my mother laughs as she shoos us inside.

So now my memory stands corrected. I used to play. When I was this age. I played. I was happy. I liked it. I smelled liked puppies. I was a puppy party.

I played.

I don't know why I ever stopped.

I suddenly find that I start asking *myself* the same question that the children ask me: *wanna play?*

Yes. Yes, I do.

But in order to do so, I know I have to make some real changes.

I make a rule that I will not work on Saturday or Sunday unless it's an emergency or unless the show is filming. I've been guilty of working straight through far too many weekends in order to "get ahead." There's no such thing. The work is always there in the morning.

I change the bottom of my email signature so that it now reads: **<u>Please Note</u>: I will not engage in work emails after 7 pm or on weekends. IF I AM YOUR BOSS, MAY I SUGGEST: PUT DOWN YOUR PHONE."** And then I do what seems impossible: I *actually stop answering emails that arrive after seven p.m.* I have to turn off my phone to do it. But I do it. I have incredibly expert people working for me who run our sets. Learning to step back and let these people have the pleasure of doing their jobs without my peering over their shoulders has been great for them and for me both.

I make a vow to come home by six p.m. every night for dinner. If an issue is happening at work, I can find a way to come home from six p.m. to eight p.m. to be with the kids and then hop on my computer and work from home after that. Technology should be making it easier and easier for this to happen.

I'm not perfect at it.

In fact, I fail as often as I succeed. But what I know now is that this downtime is helping to relight that little spark inside, it's helping my creativity and in the long run helping me tell the stories my work needs me to tell. I give myself permission to view this downtime as essential. It's hard to do. It's hard to feel like I deserve any time to replenish the well when I know everyone else is working hard too. Except once again, there's Delorse in my kitchen:

"Shonda, what happens when you get sick? What happened that time you threw your back out? That time you had the flu?"

We don't like to talk about it at work. It's like tempting fate. But Delorse means when I go down, the shows go down. If I go down, eventually things in Shondaland come to a halt. Because of that track laying that has to happen. The stories originate with my brain. And if they can't come out of my brain, no one can even begin to lay track. And if the track can't be laid, the train cannot roll. It's the same with Kerry Washington, Viola Davis, Ellen Pompeo—if one of them goes down, so goes a show. The cameras can't roll without them. It makes it incredibly essential to keep in good shape.

Ellen, who seems to have more stamina and determination than anyone I've ever seen, once said that making twenty-four episodes of network television is like running a marathon twenty-four times. Since season one, she has treated herself like an athlete in training. Ellen believes that to do her job well, she needs to take care of herself—inside and out. Ellen's approach becomes my inspiration. I decide maybe it's time I started thinking the same way about my job.

For me, that means that if track is going to be laid, I need some time to play.

Wanna play?

Home by six. No phones after seven. Try not to work weekends.

Then I expand it.

Wanna play?

I use it as a way of allowing myself to seek comforts I would not normally allow. "Wanna play?" starts to become a shorthand for indulging myself in ways I'd forgotten about.

Manicures? Pedicures?

Wanna play? YES.

Browse for hours in an actual bookstore on a Saturday afternoon when the kids are on a playdate?

Wanna play? YES.

A long bath with some Aretha Franklin blaring loud enough that no one can hear me singing?

Wanna play? HELL YES.

A glass of wine and a square of chocolate and fifteen minutes of guiltless silence with my door closed?

Wanna play? Please keep your voice down, but . . . yes.

Fifteen minutes, I say. What could be wrong with giving myself my full attention for just fifteen minutes?

Turns out?

Nothing.

The more I play, the happier I am at work. The happier I

am at work, the more relaxed I become. The more relaxed I become, the happier I am at home. And the better I get at the playtime I have with the kids.

It's really just love.

We could all use a little more love. A lot more love.

For the kids. For me.

This is the best YES.

Wanna play?

8

Yes to My Body

Here's a thing I maybe forgot to mention.

When I decide to begin my Year of Yes?

That night I decide I am going to start saying yes to the things that scare me? That night I told you about when I am lying on the sofa with a glass of wine staring at my Christmas tree?

I am fat.

I'm not cutely chubby. Or nicely plus-size.

I am not round in my rump.

I don't have junk in my trunk.

I'm not voluptuous.

I'm not going pa-*pow* and ba-*bam* in all the right places.

I'm not working my curves the way I did in college.

If I was, you can bet I would be wearing something cute and tight and daring you to say something about it.

But that is not what is going on.

No.

I am fat.

I am obese.

I am the biggest I have ever been in my entire life.

I am so fat that I am uncomfortable in my own skin. So fat that I'm having the surreal experience of catching a glimpse of myself in a mirror and wondering with genuine confusion, "Who is that?" It actually takes a few seconds for my brain to catch up, for me to realize, with shock, that I am looking at my own reflection. That stranger is me. I am staring at myself encased in many, many extra pounds of fat. So many I'm afraid to get on a scale.

I am *massive.*

But that's not the thing.

I *am* massive.

But more important . . .

. . . I *feel* massive.

Which *is* the thing.

Look. I will not be told what size to be. I do not care about anyone else's judgment about my body. I am not interested in anyone else's ideas of what I'm supposed to look like.

I believe everyone's body is theirs and everyone has a right to love their body in whatever size and shape and package it comes in. I will fight for anyone's right to do so. I will kick ass and take names if I have to. Your body is yours. My body is mine. No one's body is up for comment. No matter how small, how large, how curvy, how flat. If you love you, then I love you.

But this is not about loving me.

I don't FEEL good.

And while part of me means it emotionally, I mostly mean it physically.

I don't FEEL GOOD.

My knees hurt. My joints hurt. I discover that the reason I am so exhausted all the time is because I have sleep apnea. I am now on high blood pressure medication.

I can't get comfortable.

I can't touch my toes.

My toes are *untouchable*.

I need to eat a piece of cake to cope with this discovery.

I am a mess.

I do not know how this has happened.

Except I do.

Remember that genetic Powerball lottery the women in my family have won? The one that means we will never look older than a pack of terribly tired teenagers? It seems there's also a metabolic SuperLotto that had the winning numbers—but only for HALF the women in my family. So my sisters Delorse and Sandie have the great luck of not only looking fourteen years old but also being able to eat half a cow in one sitting and never look larger than, well, a FOURTEEN-YEAR-OLD. I, on the other hand, did not draw those numbers. Fat runs toward me and jumps up onto my body and clings there. Like it knows that it has found a home. Like it wants to be with its people.

I've battled my weight my entire life. It always seemed unfair. It was always a horrible struggle. And after a while, I decided that struggling was not worth it. So I stopped battling. I stopped starving myself. And I settled in at what seemed like a not too heavy but not skinny weight. Plus-size. Juicy. Curvy. Definitely cute. Great booty. I was healthy. I was working out. I wasn't thinking too much about my body anyway.

And then . . . I lost control of the wheel.

Don't ask me exactly when. I'm not sure.

But I know it coincided with my slowly closing all the doors of my life. Saying no to things. Shutting down.

And here's the thing. It didn't really feel like that was what was happening.

I mean, I had a lot going on.

I had some excellent excuses for letting go of that wheel.

I decided to freeze my eggs. Like, the ones inside my body. Babies. Yes! The miracle of life. In order to freeze your eggs, you have to inject yourself with some hormones. Now, if you are a naturally thin person, you seem to stay thin. If you are me . . . not so much.

Then out of nowhere, I had a minor surgery. Which made me go, "I better stop all of this working out. And maybe lie down here on this sofa for a bit to recuperate."

Um, the surgery was on my eye.

So?

What's your point?

It doesn't matter that the surgery was on my eye. My EYE needed to recuperate. But when my eye was better, that sofa kind of needed me. It didn't seem *that* important to get back up. Plus, there was some good TV on.

Oh, yes. TV. I had a job. *Grey's Anatomy.* Then I had two jobs. I added *Private Practice.* Then I had three jobs. I added *Scandal* on top of those shows. And then just as I said good-bye to *Private Practice*, we began producing *How to Get Away with Murder.* And the more shows I had, the more I could be found at my desk or on a sofa in an editing room. The more I could be found sitting on my butt. The more I sat, the less I moved.

The less I moved?

Don't make me say it . . .

And the shows were doing so well. Which was like some kind of cruel joke. If something had failed, the irony was that I would have had the time to take myself to the gym. I would have had the time to get some rest. I would have had the time to take care of myself. At least, that's the story I told myself. But nothing got canceled. I was succeeding. I was doing more than succeeding.

It's incredibly rare for a television drama to run even three seasons, and by this point, the shows I'd created had all gone at least five.

Shondaland was a brand now. The studio expected us to produce more shows. The network expected me to maintain the quality of the ones currently on the air. Now I owned an entire night of the most expensive real estate on television. TGIT had taken over social media. Everyone around me seemed invested. Very invested. I started having nightmares about getting canceled.

Delorse and Jenny McCarthy fussed over me, worrying that my creativity would be affected by stress. They didn't understand—my creativity was the one place I never felt stress. Creating worlds, characters, stories has always been where I am most at ease. With the empty whiteboard of an episode before me, I slip into a zone of calm confidence. I feel the *hum*. Making television for me is . . . blissful. I can make stuff up the way other people can sing—I have simply always been able to hit all the notes. At its core, a TV show is just a bigger pantry. So I wasn't worried about writing the shows or making the shows.

I was worried about rising expectations. I was worried about the stakes.

Oh, yeah. Maybe I should mention: there are stakes, and man oh man, are they *high*.

As the shows got more popular, I was acutely, painfully aware of what was at stake. I smiled, refused to answer the question, pretended I didn't know what reporters were asking me about when they asked about race. But you can't be raised black in America and *not* know.

This wasn't just my shot. It was *ours*.

I had to do everything right. I had to keep it all afloat. I had to run to the top of the mountain. I could not rest, I could not fall, I could not stumble, I could not quit. Failing to reach the summit was not an option. Failing would be bigger than just me. Blowing it would reverberate for decades to come. With *Grey's Anatomy*, it would mean that giving an African-American woman her own show with a cast that looked like the real world was a mistake. I proved it wasn't.

The stakes got even higher for *Scandal*. If the first network drama with an African-American leading lady in thirty-seven years didn't find an audience, who knows how long it would take for another to come along? Failure meant two generations of actresses might have to wait for another chance to be seen as more than a sidekick.

I am what I have come to call an F.O.D.—a First. Only. Different. We are a very select club, but there are more of us out there than you'd think. We know one another on sight.

We all have that same weary look in our eyes. The one that wishes people would stop thinking it remarkable that we can be great at what we do while black, while Asian, while a woman, while Latino, while gay, while a paraplegic, while deaf. But when you are an F.O.D., you are saddled with that burden of extra responsibility—whether you want it or not.

When I made my first television show, I did something I felt was perfectly normal: in the twenty-first century, I made the world of the show look the way the world looks. I filled it with people of all hues, genders, backgrounds and sexual orientations. And then I did the most obvious thing possible: *I wrote all of them as if they were . . . people.* People of color live three-dimensional lives, have love stories and are not funny sidekicks, clichés or criminals. Women are the heroes, the villains, the badasses, the big dogs. This, I was told over and over, was trailblazing and brave.

I hope you have your left eyebrow raised too, dear reader. Because—girl, please. But I was doing a thing that the suits had said could not be done on TV. And America was proving them wrong by watching. We were literally changing the *face* of television. I was not about to make a mistake *now*. You don't get second chances.

Not when you're an F.O.D.

Second chances are for future generations. That is what you are building when you are an F.O.D. Second chances for the ones who come behind you.

As Papa Pope told his daughter Olivia: "You have to be twice as good to get half as much . . ."

I didn't want half. I wanted it all. And so I worked four times as hard.

I never wanted to have to look at myself in the mirror and say that I didn't try as hard as I could to make these shows work. That I didn't give 100 percent to leave a legacy for my daughters and for all the young women of color out there who wondered what was possible. It irritated me *to my core* that we live in an era of ignorance great enough that it was still necessary for me to be a role model, but that didn't change the fact that I was one.

I got into the habit of working as hard as I could all the time. My life revolved around work. And outside of work, I took the path of least resistance. I didn't have the energy for difficult conversations or arguments. So I smiled and let people get away with treating me however they wanted. And that only made me yearn to be back in the office. Where I was in charge. Where I was the boss. Where people were too respectful or kind or happy or afraid to treat me like crap.

Because I worked so much, I found myself constantly tired. In the early days of *Grey's*, I said no to so many invitations that people actually stopped asking me. I began to have a reputation as someone who did not socialize with work people outside of work. In reality, I didn't socialize with *any-*

one outside of work. My larger circle of friends also didn't understand; there were whispers I'd abandoned them for a glamorous Hollywood life filled with parties and famous friends. I would have laughed at this, but I was just too tired. I'd get an angry email about a missed birthday and would be asleep face-first on my keyboard before I could craft an apologetic response. Finally I just . . . gave up. My friends self-selected down to a smaller core group. I stayed home more. And spent more time working. More time alone. More time hiding.

Losing yourself does not happen all at once. Losing your-self happens one *no* at a time. No to going out tonight. No to catching up with that old college roommate. No to attending that party. No to going on a vacation. No to making a new friend. Losing yourself happens one pound at a time.

The more I worked, the more stressed I was. The more stressed I was, the more I ate.

I knew things were getting out of hand. As I started to feel more uncomfortable. As I started to feel more tired. As the jeans got tighter and tighter. When I went up size after size. When I needed the largest-size clothing in the plus-size shop.

And yet.

I was ambivalent about so much of it. The feminist in me didn't want to have the discussion with myself. I resented the need to talk about weight. It felt as though I was judging myself on how I looked. It felt shallow. It felt misogynistic.

It felt . . . traitorous to care.

My body is just the container I carry my brain around in.

I started saying that back in college when the frat guys would make dirty comments about my boobs. And I used this tone. A tone that said, *God, how dumb are you?*

But I had to say it to them a lot. To make them know that I should be invisible to them. To make them stop looking.

And now I was saying it to myself a lot. To make me invisible to myself.

My body is just the container I carry my brain around in.

I said it while I ate cartons of ice cream.

I said it while I ate whole pizzas.

I said it while I enjoyed mac and cheese with bacon in it. You heard me. *Bacon* in it. I ate anything that had bacon in it. Or was wrapped in bacon. One meat wrapped in another meat clearly proved the universe was unfolding exactly as it should.

My body is just the container full of bacon that I carry my brain around in.

And maybe it is. Maybe it is just the container I carry my brain around in.

But so is a car. And if the car is broken down and busted, my brain isn't going anywhere. Same goes for my container.

I felt . . . old. Not "I'm old and I like to lie" old.

Old.

"Stop participating in the world" old.

"Sit in a chair and watch the world go by" old.

What an extraordinary waste of a life.

But what a tasty human veal . . .

I think no one is noticing. I think no one sees. I think the fact that I have doubled in size may not be that noticeable. Because I don't really notice it. It's happened so gradually. I am invisible to myself. I think I am maybe invisible to everyone.

I am not.

People tried to be tactfully helpful. People said things to me like, "Endorphins make you feel good."

So does chocolate cake, fool.

Betsy Beers, whom I love and adore and would honestly slay a dragon for (or at least kill a spider for), once said, "You just have to train yourself to love salads."

I did not speak to her for several days. Who *trains themselves to love salads*?

What kind of sicko trains themselves to love salads?! I could also train myself to love the taste of gravel. Or cow crap. But why? I don't hate myself.

I hired a trainer. And then I promptly fired him because he said, "Nothing tastes as good as thin feels!"

He clichéd at me.

He clichéd at me in a perky, condescending tone.

"Nothing tastes as good as thin feels!"

Who says that to a fat woman? Seriously? WHO SAYS THAT? Because clearly, a) you have never had barbecue ribs, and b) shut your stupid mouth.

Being tasty veal is not something I'm happy about. Even veal does not want to be veal. Veal wants to be rescued by PETA. I start to long to be rescued as well.

I get on a plane to New York. I'm a fancy TV writer. So I have a first-class ticket, a big first-class comfy seat. I settle in, shoes off, pull out my book, grab the seat belt and—

Well, it's gotta be broken.

It's BROKEN, right?

I HAVE A BROKEN SEAT BELT.

Right? RIGHT?

I do not have a broken seat belt.

I am literally too fat for a first-class airplane seat. I am Violet Beauregarde blowing up like a giant blueberry in Willy Wonka's factory. I'm the thing that ate Gilbert's grape. Poke me with a pin and I am going to pop like a balloon.

I freaking wish.

At least it would mean I wouldn't be a passenger on this plane.

The humiliation is starting to make me sweat. A sweaty Shonda is not a pretty Shonda. A sweaty Shonda is a short leap away from a hideous troll-like Shonda.

I decide that I have two choices: I can ask the flight attendant for the seat belt extender, or I can go without a seat belt, thus ensuring that karma will crash the plane and I will plummet to my death, taking hundreds of innocent seat-belt-wearing, law-abiding people with me.

You know me pretty well by now, gentle reader. What do you think I do?

Do you think I act like an adult, like a grown-ass woman who ate herself here? Do I hit that button to summon the flight attendant? Do I speak to the flight attendant in a clear and calm voice, carefully enunciating each word so everyone in the first-class cabin is sure to hear what the sweaty girl in seat 5A has to say?

"Excuse me, but it has just come to my attention that I am now way too fat for this big giant first-class airplane seat belt. May I have the very same seat belt extender that I used to smirk to myself about while thinking superior thoughts? MAY? I? PLEASE?"

Really? Me?

Please.

No.

You know me by now. You *know* I don't do that.

I choose death.

I choose death by fat and by karma and because *Catholicism don't quit*, I bravely choose to deal with the hellfire and damnation that will follow forever after as punishment for taking the rest of the plane's passengers down with me.

I toss my sweater over my lap to hide the lack of seat belt, give an apologetic smile to the man in the suit across the aisle, shut my eyes tight and wait for the painful death that is to come.

I don't die.

I'm not dead.

Hot *damn*, I'm a narcissist—did I seriously expect karma to take down a whole planeload of people because my ass got too fat and my ego got too big to admit it?

I'm alive.

But I immediately start to imagine myself dead. Imagine myself being embalmed. Imagine myself being worked on in a funeral home. Some lady putting makeup on my dead fat face. I think of the extra-large coffin. The enormous tent my sisters will have to buy to give to the funeral director to dress me in.

It sounds funny.

Not to me.

Nothing about this is funny to me.

I have two toddlers and a twelve-year-old.

What the *hell* have I been doing to myself?

I find myself wondering, "How do I *yes* this one?"

The Year of Yes, I realize, has become a snowball rolling down a hill. Each yes rolls into the next into the next and the snowball is growing and growing and growing. Every yes changes something in me. Every yes is a bit more transformative. Every yes sparks some new phase of evolution.

So what is the *Yes* here?

What do I say *Yes* to in order to get healthy?

At first, I don't know. A few days later, I'm lying in bed back at home, in the midst of a rousing session of veal practice, watching old *Doctor Who* reruns, eating chocolate-chip cookies and enjoying the raft that is my mattress when it hits me: I *like* this.

The bed.

The warm chocolate-chip cookies.

The veal practice.

The warm chocolate-chip cookies.

The TV.

The warm chocolate-chip cookies.

I like it. No. I *love* it. I'm enjoying myself. This is fun. It's easy, it's relaxing, it requires very little effort. Plus did I mention warm chocolate-chip cookies? This is a good time for me. It's a picnic. It's a party. It's a par-*tay*. This is how I roll . . .

Wait. Oh. *Oh.*

And holy crap. There it is.

I've already been saying yes.

I have been saying yes to being fat.

Which is WHY I'm now so fat. I'm not a failure; I'm *successfully* fat. I didn't let go of the wheel; I just turned the car down the fat road.

I have been saying *yes* to fatness.

And you know what? Why the hell wouldn't I? Being fat

has been easier for me. It has worked for me. I wouldn't have done it if it didn't.

Being fat made me happy.

On *Private Practice*, Naomi has the following discussion with Addison about putting food on top of feelings to make everything better:

NAOMI: I take all these feelings . . . the rage, the
          exhaustion, the sexual frustration . . . the desire
          to run Sam down with my car, the fact that
          my child now thinks her father is the good
          parent . . . I just take it all and I shove it down as
          far as it'll go. And then I just . . . put some food
          on top of it.

ADDISON: Maybe . . . you should talk to Sam instead of
          inhaling four thousand calories a day.

NAOMI: You know what? You find your magic your way,
          I'll find my magic mine.

I was finding *my* magic *my* way.

My own special formula involved red wine. And buttered popcorn. And warm chocolate cake. And anything that was fried. And five-cheese macaroni and cheese. And veal practice.

Did I tell you what veal practice is? Oh! Veal practice involved me lying very still on the sofa trying as hard as I could to mimic the life of a veal.

While eating veal.

I wish I were kidding.

It. Was. Magic.

The food created a nice topcoat. It helped to smooth down the ragged bits. Sealed off the parts of me that were broken. It filled in all the holes. Covered up the cracks. Yep, I just put some food on top of any and everything that bothered me. The food just spackled right on in there.

And presto! Underneath the food, everything inside me was smooth and cold and numb.

I was dead inside and that was good.

Magic.

Don't ever let anyone tell you that food doesn't work. Anyone who tells you that food doesn't work is either stupid or a liar or has never had food before. You can tell them I said so. It works. Putting food on top of it works. If food did not work, if it didn't work its slutty, gluttonous, more-is-more magic, everyone in America would be Angelina Jolie thin. No one would drive-thru. No one would sprinkles or pinkberry or any of it.

No.

Food *does* work. Food feels *so* good when you put it on top of all the stuff you don't want to deal with or know how to deal with. It even works on stuff you don't even recognize as worthy of dealing with.

Food is magic. It makes you feel better. It numbs you.

Beautiful magical food deadens your soul just enough so you can't think too hard about anything other than cake or sleep. Putting food on top of it casts a spell to make the feelings go away. You don't have to face yourself or think or be anything other than your brain—no body necessary.

Food works.

There's the rub.

There's the trouble.

It *works*.

I would be eating a whole bucket of fried chicken right this very minute if I thought I could still fit into these pants afterward.

If I was still okay with being dead inside.

The thing is? I'm not.

I'm not okay with being dead inside at all.

Being numb no longer suits me. It's ill-fitting and I'm antsy about it. I find myself snapping back at people more. Or writing little Bailey-esque rants into my emails when someone's upset me. I don't want to be numb. I want to tell someone who has upset me to take their attitude and shove it right up their—

Well, let's just say that I am starting to prefer it to shoving some food in my mouth on top of my hurt feelings.

What I have come to call The Airplane Seat Belt Incident of 2014 (because I am a woman who will give anything a title) has made putting food on top of it no longer an option.

After The Airplane Seat Belt Incident of 2014, I no longer can deal with being numb.

Now numb feels creepy to me.

Now numb feels not just dead but rotting.

The food doesn't spackle anymore—it suffocates.

And the moment I have this big beautiful breakthrough that changes my life?

I am *pissed off.*

The universe has ruined the comfort of my brownies and my wine. By revealing them for what they are. Because now I know the truth about them.

I feel like someone's just told the four-year-old me the truth about Santa Claus. On Christmas Eve. While I'm sitting by the fireplace. Waiting to hear the jingle bells on the roof.

Now all I'm left with are Santa's dumb elves, Ill-fitting and Antsy. Ill-fitting and Antsy are no substitute for big fat Santa Claus. Now I have to deal with this.

Now I have to say no to fatness.

Damn it. I want to kick Ill-fitting and Antsy's asses.

Losing weight is not going to be easy. Not once in my life have I ever lost more than fifteen pounds unless it involved a serious stomach flu or self-starvation to such an extent that doctors were called.

The sheer insanity of how much work it's going to be for me to push through the pain and the terror of just beginning is daunting.

Once a close friend, Jan (whose name has been changed to protect the innocent), and I checked into a fancy health spa for a week. Cal-a-Vie is a beautiful, luxurious but intense place. So intense that they tell you right up front that there is no need to bring anything—after they take your car keys, you are issued gray sweats to wear each day. Just like in the military. Or in prison. Each morning at the crack of dawn, you are driven up a mountain in a terrifying and painful death run. After that, there are three more hours of work-outs. Around noon, as you lie on the ground feeling muscles you never knew you had spasm, you whisper elaborate escape plans for getting over the wall with your fellow prisoners. But just when you've summoned the energy to make a run for it, you are retrieved by your "guide" and taken to the spa. Where, for the rest of the day, you are pampered with the most luxurious treatments known to humanity. The essence of roses that were grown and nourished with the tears of tiny baby kittens bathes your feet and you forget all about your plans to escape. Until the next morning when it starts all over again.

Ten minutes after we checked into Cal-a-Vie, Jan and I went back to the front desk. We had an emergency, we told them.

Medical.

Personal.

Vaginal, our eyebrows implied.

They gave us our car keys. We jumped in the car and drove away.

I'm not going to talk about what happened out there.

I'll *never* talk about what happened out there. I'm just going to tell you that we arrived back at the spa an hour and a half later reeking of shame and the grease of fast-food drive-thru.

We'd panicked. The fear of the oncoming diet was too much.

Now I wait for the panic. But it doesn't come. I am ready.

I get a piece of paper and tape it up on the back of my closet door. I climb on a scale. I stare at the number. I let a string of expletives that would make a sailor cry fly out of my mouth. Pen in hand, I walk back over to the paper on the back of the door. I write down the date. I write down my weight. I stare at the number. Then I rip the paper up and throw it in the trash.

I don't want to see that number ever again.

yesyesyesyesyesyesyesyesyesyesyesyesyesyesyes

I gave myself a choice. Which yes did I want to say? There were two options:

I can say yes, I want to be successful at this. I want to be healthy. I want to live a long life for myself and for my children. I want to feel good. And once I say that, I have to buckle down and do the work and not complain and accept that the work is going to be hard. Because that is what it is. Work. Hard work.

But I will be able to buckle my seat belt on the plane. I won't have narcissistic fears of a karmic plane crash. I won't have a giant coffin and wear a tent for a dress.

If I say yes, the life I save will be my own.

Or: I can say *no*. Screw losing weight.

Screw you, Skinny!

I can say I do *not* want to be successful at this. I want to eat the fried chicken. I want to be veal.

But if I say no, if I say that I do not want to do the work? Then game over. I have to shut up. I don't want to hear me whining ever again about not buckling that plane seat belt. I don't want to listen to a monologue on the pain of not touching my toes. Do not come crying to me about how I hurt my own feelings when I didn't recognize me in the mirror. Because I made a choice. I said no.

Wait.

I said yes.

I said yes to fatness.

And if I say yes to fatness, then I need to be fine if I'm rocking size 24s. I need to embrace who I am as I am. I need to buy my own seatbelt extender and pull it out of my purse, loud and proud, when I get on the plane. And dare the idiot next to me to make a comment.

The problem with the fatness isn't the fatness.

It's me.

If I am not going to change, I have to move on. I can't waste precious time hovering in the "I wishes" and the "if onlys."

That is being a dreamer. Dreamers never say yes to anything.

I HAVE TO DO.

FAT OR THIN.

I have to DO.

I don't know why I ever thought this was going to be easy. Nothing good is easy.

At work, I am a badass warrior. I'm competitive. I work hard. Hell, I'm a badass competitive warrior at croquet with my *kids*. I got competitive knitting once. KNITTING. Which is why I am not allowed to knit around other people. Sharp objects, a bloodlust for victory, balls of wool . . . it's not a good mix.

I work hard—that's how I succeed. That's how ANYONE succeeds. So why in the world did I think weight loss would be any different?

Somehow, this idea is a lightbulb for me. The idea that this is not fun—this is badass warrior work. The idea that I am NEVER going to enjoy losing weight. That I am ALWAYS going to want the fried chicken. ALWAYS. FOREVER. I will always prefer curling up on the sofa with a book to run-

ning on a treadmill. For the rest of my life, my blood will
pump a little bit faster at the scent of dark chocolate and
bacon mixed together. Cheesecake will always taste like love.
Oh, I am never going to like losing weight. Losing weight is
not fun. It will never be fun.

IT WILL BRING ME NO JOY.

IT WILL KICK MY ASS AND STOMP ME TO THE
GROUND.

Somehow, this knowledge makes me feel so much better.

The beauty of lowered expectations.

Once I stopped expecting to like it, once I stopped
demanding that losing weight be easy or pleasant, once I
stopped waiting for the band to start playing, paying attention to what went into my mouth became tolerable.

Because I wasn't waiting for it to get better.

It's NEVER going to get better. It just . . . sucks.

I said yes to losing weight on March 8, 2014.

When I stepped on the scale on March 1, 2015, I had lost
almost one hundred pounds. As I write this in the summer
of 2015, I've lost more. Unexpectedly more. Then again, anything over fifteen pounds was unexpected.

More than a few pounds.

Unexpectedly more.

But saying yes is a powerful thing.

Now. I've told you how hard it was. How much I hated it.
And how I did it anyway. And still, reader-friend, someone

among you is going to ask the question anyway. Someone among you is going to ask—

"Shonda, what diet did you go on? What program did you use?"

Did I not just say it was never going to be easy? Never going to be quick? If things were easy or quick, would there be anyone left out there who talked about struggling with their weight?

Now, I'm betting all of those big-time programs you see advertised and recommended by your doctor *work*. But only if you decide that YOU are going to do the work to make the programs work. Meaning, nothing works if you don't actually decide that you are really and truly ready to do it.

Are you ready? Here's how you know if you are ready or not: Three years ago, if someone had said something to me like "Nothing works until you are really ready for it to work," I would have force-fed them butter until they weighed one thousand pounds. Because that sounds like crap. Everything sounds like crap until you are in the right mind-set. Everything sounds like crap while you are still busy listing reasons you should get to eat that whole cake.

You *should* get to eat that whole cake. Yes. You should. And you *can*. You can eat the whole delicious cake. You just have to accept that it will make your belly fat. And that is okay. But then do not complain about having a fat belly.

Stop berating and shaming and hiding yourself. Become one with your fat belly and love your body for all its gifts. Spend your valuable years on this planet thinking about something other than your weight.

Now. Moving on to—

"But Shonda, what diet did you go on? What program did you use?"

Sigh. Fine.

I did not go on any specific diet or use any specific program. And I did not have any kind of weight-loss surgery. But I will tell you what I did. And I'm not a professional of any kind except a fake TV doctor writer, so remember that I know absolutely NOTHING about weight loss. Because I'm a WRITER. Which means I highly recommend you do the very first thing I did, which is:

1. Start by seeing a licensed physician. I went to my doctor and I said, "I don't wanna be fat anymore. Help. Me." My doctor literally applauded me. Eva's cool that way. I asked for and got a complete physical. I did this so I knew where I was starting out because I wanted to know what I was working with. I wanted to be able to see progress in even the smallest ways. *I also did whatever my doctor told me to do.*

After that:

2. I thought about exercise. I promised myself that I would never do any exercise that I did not like. So I didn't. In the beginning, I didn't exercise at all. I was too busy trying to convince myself to not eat everything I could get my hands on. But when I was ready, I called a trainer. I'd worked with Jeanette Jenkins before. Well, mostly I'd complained and wheezed while she tried to get me to move my body. Now, I was ready to do what I was told. Jeanette got me doing Pilates and I loved it. I mean, who wouldn't? It's exercise you do *lying down*. For real. It's like the universe finally decided to cut me some slack. Okay, it's also really hard. But still. YOU LIE THERE.

3. I made myself drink sixty-four ounces of water every day. Which is just A LOT of water. But it made my skin look fantastic.

4. I decided—and this was the most important rule for me—that no food was off-limits. I could eat anything I wanted. As long as I ate a reasonable portion. Also—and this was the hardest part of this important rule—I could only eat <u>exactly what I was craving</u>. Try doing that for a day. I'd been so used to eating simply because it was breakfast time or lunchtime or dinnertime—I'd never stopped to think about whether or not I was hungry, let alone *craving* anything. I had never actually listened to my body before. I know, I know: a phrase like "listen-

ing to your body" sounds suspect. Like synergy. But it
works!

The actors on my shows seemed to know what I was
doing before almost anyone else. Perhaps because as actors
their bodies are their work instruments, because they are
stared at all day, because they must be so physically present,
they could tell instantly that something had changed for
me. They got it and they seemed to understand instinctively
how hard-going my weight loss was. They were all over me
with support. Katie Lowes, Scott Foley, Kerry Washington
and Ellen Pompeo in particular felt like my weekly cheer-
leaders; every time I saw one of them at table reads, they
had some encouraging word or a hug. As I began to make
progress, Ellen told me sternly: "Be careful. Do not lose the
booty, lady." *Not possible, Ells.*

As I started to really lose weight, something interesting
started to happen. I stopped thinking of my body as a mere
container for my brain. I became more aware of it. In every
way. How it worked, how it felt, how it moved. I noticed
how the muscles in my back tightened up in response to
stress. I stretched more often. This is gonna sound weird but
I became obsessed with my skin and making it perfectly
smooth and soft. This meant a LOT of moisturizing of knees
and feet and hands before bed.

And I started to feel strong. Like, truly strong. When I

power posed now, I didn't just *feel* confident like Wonder Woman. *I felt like Wonder Woman.* Fifty pounds in, I put my daughter Emerson on my back and galloped up and down the halls of our house with her hanging on to my shoulders and squealing. After I put her down for her nap, I sat down on the steps and burst into tears. Four months ago, there was no way I would have been able to haul myself down the hall even once with a child on my back. Not even at a brisk walk. A gallop would have almost killed me. Now I wasn't even winded.

For the first time in my life, the woman who had to be dressed like a child and told to stand still to wait for Oprah began to care about clothes. Dana Asher had been my stylist for years. But dressing me for events had always been like dressing a fat mannequin—I had no opinions, I just wore the clothes. I didn't give a crap what she put on me as long as I felt invisible. Not that it mattered—the variety of clothing choices for plus-size women had always been sparse. It was depressing.

Now, I had the opposite problem. I had my pick of designers. The choices were endless. Overwhelming. But I had never shopped in the non–plus-size section of the store before. I felt awkward. I had no sense of what looked good on this new body I was now settling into. Dana literally cleared out my closets. Everything I owned down to my undies no longer fit. The good stuff went to charity. (I managed to hang on to all of my *Grey's Anatomy* T-shirts—they swam on me but I wasn't letting them go.) Not much else remained. We started over. Dana taught me how to dress, introduced me to colors I'd never considered, coaxed me into form-fitting clothes. I got to know designers. Nothing I wore made me feel invisible.

Inside this body, I now felt okay about being seen.

By men. I'd been seen before. But I wasn't paying attention to it. I was in the pantry. I was writing. I was busy hiding. And lately, I was too busy protecting myself from what had been happening to my life.

Slowly, I am coming to realize that is part of it.

The shyness.

The introversion.

The layers of fat.

I'm a quiet nerdy writer who seemingly overnight became . . . well, famous. Being famous, even if you are an actor, is considered the toll you pay for getting to do your job at the highest level.

For a writer?

The unexpected shock of it was . . . shocking. And a little bit terrifying. Most writers do not set out to become famous. They set out to sit alone in their pajamas in the back of the pantry and dream. They set out to tell stories. They set out to create worlds. That is who they are.

That is who I am.

Was.

And then lightning struck in the craziest, most amazing

way. And people began to know my name and recognize my face. And with that comes a lot of attention. From all kinds of places.

From people who never before looked in my direction. Now they were ALL looking in my direction. And they were smiling. And being nice. And offering me things.

I didn't want to be looked at. I didn't feel okay being seen. I just wanted to write and hang out with the same friends I've always had and be left alone.

How do you accomplish that in this town?

Your body becomes a container for your brain.

It was a damned good security system.

Now, though, I am seen. And I am getting comfortable being seen. I'm getting used to being seen. I am realizing that there's a part of me that *wants* to be seen.

And that it's okay to want to be seen.

That it's okay to want to be seen.

It's okay to *like* being seen.

I'm being seen.

When I walk past a mirror, it still happens. I catch a glimpse and I think, "Who *is* that?" The girl in the mirror is a size she hasn't been since she was sixteen years old. And she looks younger, like her genetic lottery ticket just won a second time around.

But it's me. I'm seeing me.

And I like what I see there.

That girl looks happy.
All it took was the right kind of yes.
And salad.
Oh, yeah. It turns out?
Betsy was right.
It does help to train yourself to love salads.
I *hate* it when she's right.

9

Yes to Joining the Club

About a year into my Year of Yes, Chris #1 calls to tell me that I'm being awarded the *Hollywood Reporter*'s Sherry Lansing Award at the annual Women in Entertainment breakfast. He keeps his tone soothingly soft, the mellow tones of a psychiatric nurse, as he informs me that I will have to give a speech.

Then he waits for me to freak out.

This speech is not your average speech. The Dartmouth commencement was a big deal, yes. But this. This is not a crowd of Dartmouth graduates looking to the future, looking for wisdom. This is not a gaggle of hopeful and happy parents just thrilled they are done paying hundreds of thousands of dollars in tuition.

It's right in the title: this speech is for women in entertainment. These are *powerful* women in entertainment. You know
how I know this? The *Hollywood Reporter* releases a list to go
with this event. It's called the Power 100.

Some of the women who will be in that room listening
to my speech are legends. Sherry Lansing *herself* will be in
that room.

Chris waits for me to start yelling. He waits for chicken-
bone-Janet-Jackson-Boob-fear-snot hollering in his ear. I'm
quiet a long moment. Then:

"Okay," I say.

"Okay?" He sounds confused. "Okay like . . . okay, fine?"

"Yeah. Okay, fine."

Chris thinks perhaps I do not understand.

"You have to *GIIIIVE A SPEEEECH*." He says it slowly.
Loudly. Like my hearing is going. Like I really *am* old.

But I heard him. And I am nervous. But it is time.

This is a room full of women. Powerful women. I am on
the list. Theoretically, I am one of these powerful women.
Theoretically, these are my peers. And yet . . .

I don't actually know a single woman on the list. What this
really is? Is a room full of strangers. Powerful strangers.

I have been enjoying this year in a way I haven't enjoyed
life in a long time. I'm excited and I'm vibrant and I'm feeling alive. I've made progress, I've gotten so much better at
this but I have no friends in the industry outside the ones

who work on my shows. Everyone I know works for me or with me. I am a powerful woman who knows no powerful women.

I am on the list but I am not *of* the list.

Chicken bone, Janet Jackson Boob, fear-snot, y'all.

I have too long been a turtle in my shell with my sisters in the industry.

It is time to stop standing at the edges of rooms. Hugging the walls. Living in my head. Wishing I had something to say. If there's one thing I have learned from all of Chris's Sisyphean pushing and all of this saying Yes it's that if I don't poke my head out of my shell and show people who I am, all anyone will ever think I am is my shell.

It is time to take my place on the list.

HOLLYWOOD REPORTER WOMEN
IN ENTERTAINMENT SPEECH

Delivered December 10, 2014
Los Angeles, California

ON CEILINGS MADE OF GLASS

When my publicist called to tell me that I was receiving this honor, I screwed up my face and I said, "Are you sure? Me?"

And he said, "Yes."

And I said, "Why?"

And then I said, "No really, WHY?"

And I made him call and ask for some written reason why I was getting this award. Because I really and truly was worried that there might have been some kind of mistake.

I want to pause for a beat here to say that I don't say these things to be self-deprecating and humble. I am not a self-deprecating, humble person. I think I'm pretty fantastic. But I also think that the *Hollywood Reporter* Sherry Lansing Award is extraordinary—as is Sherry Lansing herself.

So . . . no, really, WHY?

They sent a written reason why I was getting this award. It said many nice things but the main thing that it said was that I was getting the award in recognition of my breaking through the industry's glass ceiling as a woman and an African-American.

Well.

I call my publicist back.

Because I just don't know about this. I mean, I'm concerned now.

I come from a very large, very competitive family. *Extremely* competitive. And by *competitive*, I mean, my mother says we're not allowed to play Scrabble anymore when we get together because of the injuries and the tears. One of the rules in my family is you don't ever get a trophy for participation, you don't get a trophy for just being you. So getting an award today BECAUSE I'm a woman and an African-American feels . . .

I was born with an awesome vagina and really gorgeous brown skin.

I didn't do anything to make either of those things happen.

To get all Beyoncé about it, people: "*I woke up like this.*"

Seriously.

I know this isn't an award because I'm a woman or BECAUSE I'm African-American. I know that it's really about breaking the glass ceiling that exists in the face of being a woman and being black in this very male, very white town.

But I haven't broken through any glass ceilings.

"Do they know I haven't broken through any glass ceilings?" I ask my publicist.

He assures me that I have. I assure him that I have not.

I have not broken through any glass ceilings.

If I had broken through any glass ceilings, I would know.

If I had broken through a glass ceiling, I would have felt some cuts, I would have some bruises. There'd be shards of glass in my hair. I'd be bleeding, I'd have wounds.

If I'd broken the glass ceiling, that would mean I would have made it through to the other side. Where the air is rare. I would feel the wind on my face. The view from here—way up here where the glass ceiling is broken—would be incredible. Right?

So how come I don't remember the moment? When me with my woman-ness and my brown skin went running full speed, gravity be damned, into that thick layer of glass and smashed right through it?

How come I don't remember that happening?

Here's why:

It's 2014.

This moment right here, me standing up here all brown with my boobs and my Thursday night of network television full of women of color, competitive women, strong women, women who own their bodies and whose lives revolve around their work instead of their men, women who are big dogs? That could only be happening right now.

Think about it.

Look around this room. It's filled with women of all colors in Hollywood who are executives and heads of studios and VPs and show creators and directors. There are a lot of women in Hollywood in this room who have the game-changing ability to say yes or no to something.

Fifteen years ago, that would not have been as true. There'd have been maybe a few women in Hollywood who could say yes or no. And a lot of D girls and assistants who were gritting their teeth and working really hard. And for someone like me, if I was very very VERY lucky, there'd have been maybe one small show. One small shot. And that shot would not have involved a leading actress of color, any three-dimensional LGBT characters, any women characters with high-powered jobs AND families, and no more than two characters of color in any scene at one time—because that only happened in sitcoms.

Thirty years ago, I'd think maybe there'd be a thousand secretaries fending off their handsy bosses back at the office and about two women in Hollywood in this room. And if I were here, I would be serving those two women breakfast.

Fifty years ago, if women wanted to gather in a room . . . well, it had better be about babies or charity work. And the brown women would be in one room over there and the white women would be in another room over here . . .

From then to now . . . we've all made such an incredible leap.

Think of all of them.

Fifty years ago trying to get out of separate rooms, thirty years ago trying to not serve breakfast or be groped by their bosses, fifteen years ago trying to make clear that they could run a department as well as that guy over there.

All the women, white or black or brown, who woke up like this, who came before me in this town.

Think of them.

Heads up, eyes on the target.

Running. Full speed. Gravity be damned.

Toward that thick layer of glass that is the ceiling.

Running, full speed, and crashing.

Crashing into that ceiling and falling back.

Crashing into it and falling back.

Into it and falling back.

Woman after woman.

Each one running and each one crashing.

And everyone falling.

How many women had to hit that glass before the first crack appeared?

How many cuts did they get, how many bruises? How hard did they have to hit the ceiling? How many women had to hit that glass to ripple it, to send out a thousand hairline fractures?

How many women had to hit that glass before the pressure of their effort caused it to evolve from a thick pane of glass into just a thin sheet of splintered ice?

So that when it was my turn to run, it didn't even look like a ceiling anymore.

I mean, the wind was already whistling through—I could always feel it on my face. And there were all these holes giving me a perfect view to the other side. I didn't even notice the gravity, I think it had already worn itself away. So I didn't have to fight as hard. I had time to study the cracks. I had time to decide where the air felt the rarest, where the wind was the coolest, where the view was the most soaring. I picked my spot in the glass and I called it my target.

And I ran.

And when I finally hit that ceiling, it just exploded into dust.

Like *that*.

My sisters who went before me had already handled it.

No cuts. No bruises. No bleeding.

Making it through the glass ceiling to the other side was simply a matter of running on a path created by every other woman's footprints.

I just hit at exactly the right time in exactly the right spot.

So I'm breaking my family's rule today.

This is a trophy for participation.

And I am beyond honored and proud to receive it.

Because this? *Was a group effort.*

Thank you to all the women in this room.

Thank you to all the women who never made it into this room.

And thank you to all the women who will hopefully fill a room one hundred times this size when we are all gone.

You are all an inspiration.

10

Yes, Thank You

I was at a dinner celebrating women in TV hosted by *Elle* magazine and its editor in chief, Robbie Myers. It was one of the YES events I'd made an agreement with myself to attend. In the beginning of the Year of Yes, I dreaded these events. Small talk, nerves, photographers—it was all too much, it made my brain freeze. But by this point, deep into the year, I found myself almost looking forward to these events. I was almost comfortable. I smiled for the photographers and made my way down the press line into the event, where I actually managed to exchange intelligent small talk with talented writers and actors I had long admired.

Breathe in, breathe out.

I no longer had that horrible sinking feeling that I always had at parties. That sad, runny-nose-pressed-to-the-cold-glass feeling of not belonging.

There were no longer disturbing silences where people stared at me, waiting for me to speak. I no longer did the thing where I tried to stand as still as a marble statue in the hopes that freezing my form would magically render me invisible to the naked eye. I was blessedly no longer worried about flinging a chicken bone across the room.

And I only needed one pair of Spanx at a time these days. They were still too tight. But still. Progress.

I actually found myself thinking, "This is going to be a great evening."

Before dinner was served, Robbie Myers welcomed us. She was smart and funny as she called out each name and pointed all of us out. Then, explaining why they were chosen for the magazine's list of great women in TV, she named each woman's accomplishments.

The accomplishments were innovative, bold and impressive. A staggering number of powerful, accomplished women sat at that table.

And yet, as the editor in chief pointed to each woman and named her powerful achievements, without fail—

—*without fail*—

—every single woman named did one of three things:

1. Shook her head and looked away, waving off the words and ensuing applause as if to say, "No. Nooo. Not really. Look. It's not as great as she's telling you. I maybe really was just mopping the floors and I tripped and fell, and accidentally typed that whole script."

2. Ducked her head, an embarrassed look on her face: "Me? She's talking about me? Don't talk about me, nobody should ever talk about me. Talk about someone else." If there were any kind of cheers when her name was called, she covered her face with her hands. Almost as though she was trying to shield herself from a tragedy unfolding before her.

3. Laughed. A mortified, embarrassed, stunned "I can't believe I'm even sitting at this table with all of these awesome people because what she is saying about me is the world's biggest lie but they let me in the door anyway" laugh. Everything about her says, "WOW. Just . . . WOW."

I chose Door Number Two.

Robbie Myers rattled off a list of all the things that I'd done, all the work, all the ways I'd changed how women are portrayed on TV, how people of color are portrayed on TV. And I ducked my head down, shaking my head. Covering my face with hands. Waiting for the attention and applause to go away.

Nothing to see here, folks. Move on.

Door. Number. Two.

But when the editor in chief sat down next to me and very pleasantly said something like, "Now, where are you from, Shonda? Ohio, is it?"

I responded with, "Did you notice not a single woman in this room can handle being told she is awesome? What is *wrong* with us?!"

The editor in chief blinked. I was not engaging in the rules of dinner conversation, which requires you to start with small talk. To start by wading in. I just leapt right into the deep end of the pool.

She blinked. And then she smiled.

And then we had one of the most honest and interesting conversations I've ever had with a complete stranger while suffering a deficit of oxygen to my brain due to the tightness of my Spanx.

But it stuck with me.

Bugged me.

Itched the back of my neck.

Not a single woman in the room could handle being told, "You're awesome." I couldn't handle being told I am awesome. What in the hell is *wrong* with us?

I didn't have any answers.

And not having any answers, I did what I was now starting to do in these situations.

I decided to YES it.

Which is what I was finding myself doing more and more frequently.

Instead of wallowing in the problem, I figure out what its YES would be.

Sometimes this ends up being a ridiculous mind game. But most of the time it works.

The point of this whole Year of Yes project is to say yes to things that scare me, that challenge me. So in order to YES a problem, I have to find whatever it is inside the problem that challenges me or scares me or makes me just *freak out*—and then I have to say yes to *that thing*.

Which feels like counterintuitive insanity.

But, I'm slowly coming to understand, it's not insanity. I race into the wilderness and it's all darkness and thorny bushes and rocky uphill paths and I am spitting out swear words left and right and then suddenly—

I break through into the clearing and find I'm standing on the mountaintop. Air in my lungs. Sunlight on my face.

It's not insanity. It's just tough.

It's like surgery. You can't close the patient's chest until you've found the wound and operated on it. The problem is the open chest, the wound is the challenge and the YES is the operation.

You are making fun of me and my metaphor right now, aren't you?

You are. I can feel it.

Cut me some slack.

I've spent TWELVE SEASONS writing *Grey's Anatomy*, people. I can CBC, CHEM-7, type, cross and match you in my sleep. Do you know how to diagnose appendicitis? Fever and tenderness over McBurney's point. The common causes of post-op fever? The five Ws—wind, water, walking, wounded and wonder drugs.

If you went into labor right now? I could perform a C-section on you.

You don't want me to.

But I could.

And as any one of my writers who has been pregnant will tell you, I *would*.

The point is, my metaphors are medical.

The point is also that if you pass out in front of me, I will crack your chest and put you on an LVAD and start calling you Denny.

So maybe try to stay conscious around me.

Say yes to staying conscious.

Anyway.

I decide to do it. I decide that if it is so hard to own up to my own accomplishments, to take a compliment, to not duck my head and choose Door Number Two, then I'm going to say YES to accepting any and all acknowledgments of personal fabulous awesomeness with a clear, calm "Thank you" and a confident smile and nothing more.

I'm going to say YES and just . . . see what happens.

It sounds much easier than it is.

Someone says, "I love your show."

You know what I say back?

I say, "Oh my God, I'm just so lucky. Really fortunate. It's not me, it's everyone who works with me."

Okay. Look.

Everyone who works with me? They are AMAZING. I truly am surrounded by people—actors, line producers, directors, set decorators, costume designers, assistant directors, grips, craft service people, Teamsters, writers, so many people—who are incredibly talented and without whom Shondaland would literally not exist. There are a bunch of cool people at ABC who are pretty essential too. My agent, Chris. My lawyer, Michael. A *lot* of people make Shondaland the creative, happy and successful place that it is.

So it IS everyone who works with me.

But why am I running around saying it's NOT me?

Because it is.

It's me.

It's me *and* it's them.

It's US.

And what the hell is up with the "I'm just so lucky" line?

I'm not merely lucky.

No one who succeeds is merely lucky.

Not in the "she tripped and fell right onto a television ratings chart" way.

Lucky implies I didn't do anything. *Lucky* implies something was given to me. *Lucky* implies that I was handed something I did not earn, that I did not work hard for.

Gentle reader, may you *never* be lucky.

I am not lucky.

You know what I am?

I am smart, I am talented, I take advantage of the opportunities that come my way and I work really, really hard.

Don't call me lucky.

Call me a *badass*.

yesyesyesyesyesyesyesyesyesyesyesyesyesyesyesyes

Okay. Now, I'm going to admit something to you.

That was all an act.

There is a part of my brain that is SCREAMING at me right now for giving myself all these compliments. Screaming and wringing her brainy little hands and nervously hopping around.

"You cannot say that out loud! People will think you believe that you are . . ."

That I'm what?

Into myself.

Cocky. Immodest. Brazen.

In love with myself.

That I think I'm special.

Shudder. Shake. Hop.

FLIP OUT.

I wrote that whole series of compliments to myself as part of my YES. And it was HARD to do. I felt like a complete jerk the whole time I was writing it. And the sad part is? Right up until I got to "badass"? Those weren't even compliments.

They were facts.

Sadder?

Did I just say that I'm actually worried that people will think that I am *into myself*? I am worried that people will think that maybe *I think I am special*? That I am *in love with myself*?

Wait.

Isn't that the GOAL? Don't people pay money to licensed therapists to get into themselves, to fall in love with themselves, to think they are special?

Now, let's all put our Gloria Steinem cashmere thinking caps on and see if we can decipher this puzzler: *what is the opposite of a cocky, immodest, brazen woman?*

Anyone?

A meek, chaste, timid woman.

Who in the name of Ruth Bader Ginsburg and Queen Bey wants to be a meek, chaste, timid woman?!

Do YOU? Because I sure as hell don't.

I'm *outraged*.

But I still can't take a compliment.

And neither can any of the other women I know.

You know what? I don't think we've been raised to do so.

yesyesyesyesyesyesyesyesyesyesyesyesyesyesyesyes

Mindy Kaling went to Dartmouth College. I went to Dartmouth College. Actually, there's kind of a cool mafia of Hollywood women who went to Dartmouth. Connie Britton. Rachel Dratch. Aisha Tyler.

What? Five is *too* a mafia.

That's not the point. The point is that one day, I'm sitting around minding my own business when a member of the mafia whom I don't actually know but whose TV show I obsessively watch calls me up. For reals.

Mindy Kaling is on the phone.

Now, to be clear, I don't watch a lot of TV during the TV season. Because I'm working. But Mindy Kaling's show was something that I watched in real time, when it aired, and I tried never to miss it.

Mindy Kaling is *on the phone.*

And she is asking if I will come and do a cameo on her show, *The Mindy Project.*

Like act.

Like an actor.

Act like an actor on her show.

The show that I watch in real time when it airs and never miss.

The one that stars Mindy Kaling.

This is a joke, right?

I am being filmed and later this will be on the internet

and people will laugh at me. All my high school terrors are coming true. It's definitely a joke.

But it's not. She means it.

Mindy Kaling is *serious*.

She wants me to come and act on *The Mindy Project*.

Not give a speech.

Not be a talk show guest.

Be an actor.

Acting.

Playing a fictional version of myself, yes. But still . . .

Acting. On TV.

I don't really have a choice. I'm doing the Year of Yes.

Also? I am in love with her show.

But also?

Mindy is a Dartmouth sister. A member of the mafia.

And Mindy is an F.O.D.

First. Only. Different.

I wonder how many questions she gets about being an Indian-American woman. Probably as many questions as I get about being an African-American woman.

As an African-American woman, how does it feel to *fill in the blank*?

Here's a tip. The answer, no matter how you fill in that blank, is always the same: I don't know. Since I've never been anything other than a black woman, I can't tell you how specifically anything feels any more than someone could tell someone how things feel as a white woman. It's a creepy question. Stop asking it.

I'm betting Mindy hates the F.O.D. thing as much as I do. I say yes.

Immediately after I say yes, I become terrified about the entire thing. I think about all the ways I can cancel. I think about getting a serious illness. The third Chris in my life (if you are keeping track, we have Publicist Chris and Godfather Chris), my agent, Chris Silbermann, says there is no way I can cancel. He says that I said I would do it and he told them I would do it. He says I am doing it. He says this very firmly.

I think Publicist Chris and Agent Chris have been talking. Remind me to do something about that.

Why am I so scared?

I'm not worried about panicking during filming. I survived shooting *Kimmel* for a full hour. I can survive a few takes without hyperventilating.

I'm not worried about being on set and the cast and crew being mean or making fun of me. TV crews are notoriously great people and no one ever makes fun of guests on set anyway.

I'm worried about what will happen when it airs.

Not because of my acting skills. I don't think anyone is going to watch me act and say, "My God, Meryl Streep had better hang it up right now because here comes Shonda!" I don't even think they are going to say that Joe at the com-

munity theater should hang it up. But I know I won't completely shame myself. Well . . . I might shame myself but I
have some TV shows, people. I understand the magic that can
happen in an editing room. If I cover *The Mindy Project* set in
shame, the producers of the show will kindly hide it in editing. And then, if they are wise, use the footage to blackmail
me for the rest of my life.

I am worried that people will be whispering: *"Who does
she think she is, acting on a TV show? What, does she think she's
all that? Does she have that high an opinion of herself? My, aren't
we just a little in love with ourselves these days?"*

You heard me.

I am scared people will think I like myself too much.

yes yes yes yes yes yes yes yes yes yes yes yes yes yes yes yes

I am on Twitter, checking in on the world, and I see a tweet
from some motherhood site. It says: *"Sleeplessness is a badge of
honor for moms."*

What?

A badge of honor?

Right then and there, my hair catches on fire. My hair just
lights up in flames of instant rage. The rage may be especially
bad because I still have some PTSD from my oldest child's
infant days.

My perfect beautiful miracle baby?

Never slept. EVER. Never.

So neither did I.

Twelve years later the memories of those nights, of that sleep deprivation, still make me rock back and forth a little bit. You want to torture someone? Hand them an adorable baby they love who doesn't sleep.

Badge of honor?

Necessary evil, yes. Pain in the ass, yes.

Badge of honor?

Are you freaking kidding me? Who believes that crap? Who is drinking THAT crazy Kool-Aid?

But a lot of people are. MOST people are.

I don't think it ever occurred to me before how much and how often women are praised for displaying traits that basically render them invisible. When I really think about it, I realize the culprit is the language generally used to praise women. Especially mothers.

"She sacrificed everything for her children . . . She never thought about herself . . . She gave up everything for us . . . She worked tirelessly to make sure we had what we needed. She stood in the shadows, she was the wind beneath our wings."

Greeting card companies are built on that idea.

"Tell her how much all the little things she does all year long that seem to go unnoticed really mean to you."

With a $2.59 card.

Mother's Day is built on that idea.

This is *good*, we're told. It's *good* how Mom diminishes and martyrs herself. The message is: mothers, you are such wonderful and good people because you make yourselves smaller, because you deny your own needs, because you toil tirelessly in the shadows and no one ever thanks or notices you . . . this all makes you AMAZING.

Yuck.

What the hell kind of message is that?

Would ANYONE praise a man for this?

Those are not behaviors anyone would hope to instill in their daughters, right?

Right?

I'm not saying MOTHERHOOD shouldn't be praised. Motherhood should be praised. Motherhood is wonderful. I'm doing it. I think it's great.

There are all kinds of ways and reasons that mothers can and should be praised. But for cultivating a sense of invisibility, martyrdom and tirelessly working unnoticed and unsung? Those are not reasons.

Praising women for standing in the shadows?

Wrong.

Where is the greeting card that praises the kinds of mothers I know? Or better yet, the kind of mother I was raised by?

I need a card that says: "*Happy Mother's Day to the mom who taught me to be strong, to be powerful, to be independent, to be competitive, to be fiercely myself and fight for what I want.*"

Or "*Happy Birthday to a mother who taught me to argue when necessary, to raise my voice for my beliefs, to not back down when I know I am right."*

Or *"Mom, thanks for teaching me to kick ass and take names at work. Get well soon."*

Or simply *"Thank you, Mom, for teaching me how to make money and feel good about doing it. Merry Christmas."*

Where are the greeting cards for the kind of mother I try to be? For the kind of mother I need my kids to see? For the kind of mother I want my daughters to one day be?

And if there's no greeting card, what is there?

There is me.

I have to be my own greeting card. And to do that, I have to at least be able to take a compliment.

yesyesyesyesyesyesyesyesyesyesyesyesyesyesyesyes

The first time I try to do it, it's pathetic.

"That is a nice color on you."

I'm in an elevator. Just me and one other person. A nice-looking man. He's smiling at me. *Why* is the guy smiling at me?

I'm notoriously bad at knowing when someone is flirting with me. Later, my friend Gordon will tell me, "Fool. He was flirting with you. He was trying to meet with your client." "Meet with your client" is Gordon-speak for getting laid. See, the client is my—

Moving on.

I stare at this nice-looking man who maybe wants a client meeting. Confused. He raises an eyebrow.

Speak, Shonda, speak.

Finally I get it together.

"What?"

That's what I say to him. And my "what" is not a cute, flirty two-syllable up-talk-at-the-end "Wha-aaat?" My "what" is a flat construction-worker-get-back-to-work grunty "WHAT."

The potential client-meeter looks taken aback.

"That is a nice color on you, I said."

I look down at my dress. It's cerulean blue. I only know that it's cerulean blue because Meryl Streep gave a breathtaking monologue on the color in *The Devil Wears Prada*.

I love Meryl Streep's work. I know everyone does. But I really do. More than you. I love Meryl's work so much that no matter what role she is playing, I'm rooting for her character. So while many people think that *The Devil Wears Prada* is about how mean that boss lady is, I know they are wrong. To me, it's clear that it is a daring exposé on how hard it is to find a good assistant. Meryl, by the way? Probably knows how to take a compliment. Go Meryl and your cerulean blue.

I actually pretty much thought all of that while standing in the elevator with this man. This client-meeter. You can see why I have a hard time with small talk.

But my dress is cerulean blue and he likes it. He likes it on me.

Wait.

He said he likes it.

And I realize this is it. It's happening. My chance.

Say it. Just say thank you. Then smile. And don't say anything else. Don't offer any words of apology or remorse for
having the audacity to wear a dress someone could like. Just
stand there, confident and bold. Like you, too, think this
color is great on you.

"Thank you," I reply.

Good. Smile, Shonda. Shut up, Shonda.

I force myself to smile. Which is where things really go
wrong.

I think maybe my mouth is really dry or I'm nervous or
I am so determined to do this right that my smile comes
out . . . well, terrifying.

Like a Buffalo Bill smile. Not the cowboy Buffalo Bill.
The Buffalo Bill from *The Silence of the Lambs* who made
you put the lotion on your skin or else you'd get the hose
again.

That smile. A horrifying, stretched, ghoulish clown face is
what he must be seeing because now this nice guy who was
probably flirting with me moments earlier is pressing into
the corner of the elevator away from me like I have become
a zombie who wants to eat his face.

So instead of leaving it alone . . . Instead of being all,
"Whatever, do better next time" . . . Instead of letting a

chicken bone be a chicken bone, I try to explain to this poor man.

"That was freaky, right? The face? I was smiling. But I was totally not doing it right because I say yes to compliments now but I'm still not used to it and you are kind of the first one, the test case, and I wasn't expecting it here in this elevator, you know, ha ha, so when you said the nice thing about the color, which is cerulean blue by the way, I just kinda—"

DING.

And the doors open and the really nice cute guy who likes this color on me runs for his life from the crazy lady in the elevator. To my credit, I don't chase after him and continue trying to explain. Believe me, I want to. But I can't. I am on my way to my gynecologist's office.

Dr. Chein needs to meet with my client.

A half hour later, Dr. Chein (well, I call her Connie because I say that I must be on a first-name basis with anyone who gets to be inside me), *Connie*, is down between my thighs; my feet are up in stirrups. She's got her whole speculum swab thing going on and right now she's shining a light right up my vajayjay looking at who the hell knows what. Maybe she will find my dignity in there.

"You have a good uterus!" Connie exclaims.

I push myself up to rest on my elbows and look down at her.

"Thank you, Connie," I say. Then I smile. Then I don't say anything else.

Not to brag or anything but *that* is how it's done, folks.

yes **yes** *yes* **yes** *yes* **yes** *yes* **yes** *yes* **yes** *yes* **yes** *yes* **yes** *yes* **yes**

As the weeks roll by, this part—thank you, smile, shut up— gets easier. It takes some practice but I slowly start to get better at it.

Thank you, smile, shut up.

And what happens is, when I give myself permission to just hear the compliments and not apologize for the compliments or brush them off or negate the compliments?

I start to appreciate the compliments.

The compliments mean something to me.

More important? The fact that someone paused to take the time to give me a compliment means something to me.

No one is obligated to compliment you.

They do it out of kindness.

They do it because they want to.

They do it because they believe the compliment they are offering.

So when you negate someone's compliment, you are telling them they are wrong. You're telling them they wasted their time. You are questioning their taste and judgment.

You are insulting them.

If someone wants to compliment you, let them.

But that's not enough. That's not, I am starting to realize, even the point.

It's like the Wonder Woman pose.

Thank you, smile, shut up is good. It's good for you.

But it's a pose.

It's a fake-it-until-you-make-it.

It's not *real*.

I can stand and pose like Wonder Woman all day long but that doesn't make me Wonder Woman. Because when her hands came off her hips and she walked away, Wonder Woman never said to her friend, "No, gosh, I'm not a hero. The way the world got saved was totally just luck. I hardly did anything. I mean, if I didn't have the lasso and these bracelets, I'd be totally lost . . . I'm mean, I'm just a six-foot-tall Amazon girl with a dream."

Wonder Woman would kill that version of herself. She'd run over that meek, chaste Wonder Woman embarrassment with her invisible plane.

Wonder Woman does not fake it.

Wonder Woman is a study in *badassery*.

It's a word.

Badassery.

I know it is a word because I just typed it twice, and when my computer asked if I wanted to <u>ignore it</u> or <u>add it to my dictionary</u>? I chose <u>add it to my dictionary</u>. A word that is in the dictionary is definitively a word.

Badassery.

It's a word. The dictionary kinda sorta said so.

Badassery:

1. (noun) the practice of knowing one's own accomplishments and gifts, accepting one's own accomplishments and gifts and celebrating one's own accomplishments and gifts; 2. (noun) the practice of living life with swagger : SWAGGER (noun or verb) a state of being that involves loving oneself, waking up "like this" and not giving a crap what anyone else thinks about you. *Term first coined by William Shakespeare.*

Wonder Woman is not faking it. Wonder Woman means it. Wonder Woman is all swagger and badassery.

Compliment Wonder Woman and she'd be all, "Yeah, I'm a hero. Yeah, I saved the world. What's next?"

Wonder Woman isn't worried that her friend is going to feel bad. Wonder Woman isn't concerned people will think that she thinks she's better than they are.

Because guess what?

When it comes to using a lasso and magic bracelets and flying an invisible plane? Wonder Woman *is* better than they are. She's freaking Wonder Woman. Have you seen her boots?

If Serena Williams tells a reporter something like, "I am the best tennis player you will see in your lifetime," I am betting she isn't worried that people will think she's better than they are at tennis. Because she's SERENA WILLIAMS.

That's swagger. That is badassery.

Want more examples?

Do you think Oprah doesn't know she's the best talk show host ever? Do you think that she stays awake at night worried people think she thinks she's the best? No. And Audra McDonald and her record-setting six Tony Awards cannot possibly show up to rehearsal nervous that someone will think she believes she is a better Broadway performer, right?

I feel like Julia Child swaggered her booty off.

Taylor Swift. All kinds of young badassery.

Bey. Malala. Mo'ne Davis. The first female Army Rangers. Misty Copeland.

Just saying.

And I think this is the thing: everyone's got some greatness in them.

You do. That girl over there does. That guy to the left has some. But in order to really mine it, you have to own it. You have to grab hold of it. You have to believe it.

Serena's not worried her friend is gonna feel bad she's not as good at tennis as Serena is. You know why? Because in order to be as good as Serena, you have to decide that your goal is that NO ONE is going to be as good as you are at tennis.

Then you have to make it true.

And you have to be okay with being better than everyone else.

One of the most surprising things about *Grey's Anatomy's* becoming a big hit was how unhappy it made me.

How scared and sad and nervous. And ashamed.

My father used to tell us, "The only obstacle to your success is your own imagination." He said it so much that I hear his voice sometimes in my sleep.

Of course he was right.

But once success came, I did not know what to make of it. Many of my friends were struggling writers. Suddenly I was no longer one of them. I was on the outside looking in. I was unsure of what this change would mean. I wanted everything to stay the same.

I didn't feel like it was okay to celebrate. It's fine to be competitive when you are all on the same playing field but when you are the only one allowed in the game . . .

I took my trophies and I tucked them in the back of a cabinet and I didn't talk about the show with anyone who didn't work on the show. Ever. If someone brought it up, I shrugged it off. Ducked my head. Waved my hand.

No, don't look at me. This lasso? These bracelets? They're nothing.

I was so excited about my job. I was in love with television. In love with the magic of it. The pace, the excitement. The creativity. I wrote, "INTERIOR OPERATING ROOM—DAY," and they built an operating room. Magic.

The day after the OR was completed, I spent the entire afternoon in that operating room alone, playing. It was the pantry all over again.

I grabbed paddles and yelled, "Clear!"

I waved my arms and shouted, "Damn it, Richard, we have to save him! Clamp!"

Dream come true.

But when I wasn't at work, it was like it didn't exist. I shoved it all down. It was like this dirty little secret. The phrase "hide your light under a bushel" comes to mind. And the more I shoved it down, the more dirty it seemed. The unhappier I got.

I did not know how to celebrate my success in the face of my friends' continued struggles. I worried that they would think I thought that I was a better writer than they were. I put a lot of food on top of it trying to deal with this problem. And by the way? Fatness made for a really nice balance. Fat and successful seemed much less threatening.

Years went by. More shows were born.

And outside of the office, I kept it up.

"I'm *just* a writer."

I said that a lot. It was my folksy answer to everything. My way of making sure people knew that I didn't think that I was doing anything special. My way of not being arrogant or snotty.

"I'm *just* a writer."

Not an ounce of badassery here.

No swagger in sight.

I still couldn't own being powerful. I tried hard to make myself smaller. As small as possible. Tried not to take up space or make too much noise. Every time I won an award or something big happened, I worked to appear a little bit sillier and sweeter and simpler in the face of my own greatness.

I just wanted everyone else to feel comfortable.

Funny thing is, no one ever asked me to do it.

It just seemed like what I was supposed to do.

Like what you do.

"I'm *just* a writer."

If I am not enjoying all of this success, then see? It isn't such a big deal. I clearly don't think I'm special. I clearly am not loving myself.

Yeah.

I clearly was NOT loving myself. Everyone would agree about that.

I don't know that I ever would have changed. If Delorse hadn't said her six words and this Year of Yes hadn't happened.

So, yes.

I can take a compliment now. Thank you. Smile.

But now I've got this new goal. I want it.

Badassery.

I want to feel free to swagger.

I decide, *Yes, it is okay to go for it*.

"It's not bragging if you can back it up," I whisper to myself in the shower every morning. That is my favorite Muhammad Ali quote. If you ask me, Ali invented modern-day swagger.

I launch myself on a course toward full-fledged badassery.

People around me notice the change immediately.

My three closest friends enjoy analyzing it.

Scott tells me that it is startling to observe. He tells me that I talk more. That I used to be silent. That he likes this in me.

Zola declares, "Your whole energy has changed. The way you fill a room has changed."

Gordon tells me I look happy. And younger. He thinks my client will have more meetings.

I can certainly feel the difference. It is both terrifying and exhilarating. Mentally, I'm trying to be as cocky and immodest and brazen as I can. I'm trying to take up as much space as I need to take up. To not make myself smaller in order to make someone else feel better. I'm allowing myself to shamelessly and comfortably be the loudest voice in the room.

I'm never merely lucky.

I try hard to think I am special, to be in love with myself, to be into myself.

I strive for badassery.

Men do it all the time. Take the compliment and run. They don't make themselves smaller. They don't apologize for being powerful. They don't downplay their accomplishments.

Badassery, I'm discovering, is a new level of confidence—in both yourself and those around you. I now feel like I can see so many amazing things about myself and the people around me. It's as if before, by hiding and worrying and being unhappy, I was not looking at the people around me and seeing how truly gifted and amazing they are. There was certainly nothing in me that could have been positive and uplifting or inspiring to them. Not when I was so busy hiding and trying to be smaller and a nothing.

I've started to think we are like mirrors. What you are gets reflected back to you. What you see in yourself, you may see in others, and what others see in you, they may see in themselves.

That's deep.

Or it's stupid.

Whatever it is, it still all comes down to Wonder Woman. You stand like that, in that pose, and after a while, you start to feel like Wonder Woman and people start to look at you and SEE Wonder Woman and oddly, that makes them feel better when they are around you.

People like being around whole, healthy, happy people.

yesyesyesyesyesyesyesyesyesyesyesyesyesyesyesyesyes

I was lying in the grass the other day watching my two youngest girls, Emerson and Beckett, race around. They're wearing these light blue gauzy *Frozen* superhero capes that my sister Delorse made for them. Now, I know there are no superheroes in *Frozen* but I have been experiencing an existential crisis about Princesses and feminism and normalizing the images my daughters see and why all the girls' superhero underwear in the stores is pink when no superhero costumes are pink and—

Look, they're wearing light blue gauzy *Frozen* superhero capes because I have told them that Anna is a junior superhero with a black sister and a gay brother—both of whom are off ruling other countries because, y'know, they have jobs. You do your mothering your way. I'll do my mothering mine.

Emerson is making plane noises. Beckett is spinning and spinning and racing around with her chubby not-quite-two-year-old arms in the air, her curly hair flying. Then Beckett pauses. She looks at me.

"Mama," she says, grinning. Beckett is always grinning.

"Mama, I am mmm-credible."

Emerson pauses long enough to shout a correction.

"IN-credible! And I am MAZING!"

And then?

They swagger away.

Beckett goes back to spinning. Emerson goes back to her plane noises. Their blue gauzy capes sail in the wind.

Would that we were all two and three years old, I think.

They never apologize for their marvelousness. They do not make themselves smaller for anyone. And they too make up their own words.

That is some mazing mmcredible badassery.

I burst out laughing. I was happy.

I *am* happy.

yesyesyesyesyesyesyesyesyesyesyesyesyesyesyesyes

When it comes time to film my part on *The Mindy Project*, I am ready. I put on all the swagger I've got. I rub myself all over with badassery. And then I head down to the set. What happens next is a whirlwind. I am standing with my favorite actors in a room filled with Dartmouth paraphernalia. The experience of being both in college and inside my TV set at the same time is surreal. I'm told to say a line here and stand there. To look here and go there. Move this way and that. I try very hard to be obedient and do what I'm told. I suddenly have a renewed respect for how hard acting in front of the camera is. I also realize that as a writer I truly do not know what goes down on my soundstages. I have fun. I laugh. They are incredibly kind to me. Ike Barinholtz, who is both the head writer and an actor on the show, becomes my most favorite person ever. I get to take a photo with everyone.

I leave with a smile on my face.

I don't think I'll ever act again. But if this was my only experience, it was a perfect one.

When the episode airs, I do the boldest thing, so full of badassery and swagger. I sit down in the middle of my family room; I turn on my TV. And in real time, I watch *The Mindy Project*. I do not flinch when I see myself. I do not think, "Who does that girl think she is?"

I look myself up and down and I think, "Not bad. Actually kinda mazing and mmcredible."

Then I put on my blue *Frozen* superhero cape and I do some spinning.

Well, I do the adult version of that. Which means that I open a great bottle of wine and pour myself a glass.

yesyesyesyesyesyesyesyesyesyesyesyesyesyesyesyes

Around the same time, my assistants give me a gift. They know that I am a political fan the way some people are football fans or baseball fans. I've watched C-SPAN and called it a good time. Election night is my Super Bowl and I have been in front of the TV for wall-to-wall coverage of every Inauguration Day since I was a teenager. That President Bill Clinton was on *The Ellen DeGeneres Show* and said something extremely nice about loving everything I did in terms of my TV work was a big deal.

I tear the paper off the beautifully wrapped gift. Inside is a T-shirt.

The T-shirt reads: *Bill Clinton Loves ANYTHING I Do.*

In big bold letters.

I love this T-shirt so much that I actually scream with glee when I see it. It's perfect. But it is not for the faint of heart. That shirt is downright *cheeky*. That shirt takes courage. That shirt takes swagger. It took a lot for me to wear that shirt out of the house. Much badassery was needed.

I put it on and wore it out and about for a full day. And when anyone made a comment about it, nice, snarky or otherwise, I had only one response:

"Thank you." Smile. Shut up.

Now, if you will excuse me, I have to go lock Door Number Two. I've gotta go, you see. It is half past Swagger O'Clock and I'm late for my applause.

A NOTE ABOUT TIME

Yes to More Year of Yes

I'm well into 2015 when I realize that the Year of Yes should have ended several months ago.

The concept of ending my Year of Yes leaves me with a hollow feeling. I walk around for a few days thinking maybe I'm coming down with something. As I get ready for bed that night, I realize that what I am coming down with is a very bad case of fear.

I am only just beginning to understand that the very act of saying yes is not just life-changing, it is lifesaving. I now see two paths—a ragged rocky one that goes up to the top of the mountain and a nice easy one that heads down under it. I can fight to make the rocky climb, get a few bruises, risk getting hurt. And I can stand on the mountaintop and breathe the rare air in the warm sun, taking in the whole world before me. Or I can take the easy route underground. There's no sun down there. No air. But it's warm. It's safe. Oh hey, and there's a big supply of shovels. But really there's no need to work that hard. The dirt is nice and soft; if I just curl up on the ground, I'll slowly sink deep enough to form my own grave.

The years and years of saying no were, for me, a quiet way to let go. A silent means of giving up. An easy withdrawal from the world, from light, from life.

Saying no was a way to disappear.

Saying no was my own slow form of suicide.

Which is crazy. Because I do not want to die.

As I lie in bed later, I realize that I don't want to be done with my Year of Yes. I am a work in progress. I've just figured out how to have a little swagger. I can't stop now. I don't want to stop now. Do I have to stop now?

What began as a small challenge from my sister over chopped onions on Thanksgiving morning has become a life-or-death endeavor. I am now almost afraid to say the word *no*. I can no longer answer any challenge with *no*. That word is no longer an option for me. I know that I can't afford to say it—the cost is much too high. The fear that I may slide back down to the bottom of that mountain, the knowledge of how *easy* it would be to do so, how comfortable life at the bottom of that mountain is . . . well, that is enough to keep the word *no* from my lips.

I can experience life or I can give up on it.

What would happen if I gave up again? Who would I become? How long would it take me to begin to climb again? *Would* I even have it in me to begin to climb again? Or would that be my ending?

I'm not ready for that. I can't end. This is not the end.

This isn't the finish line.

I'm *unfinished*.

And so, no matter how much I want to, I can no longer allow myself to say no. *No* is no longer in my vocabulary. *No* is a dirty word.

Time was up.

The year was done.

But I was not.

Which is how the Year of Yes went from twelve months to forever.

I can do that.

I can change the challenge if I want to.

It's mine.

Besides, I'm not running on regular time anymore anyway.

Have you checked my clock?

I am fully synced up with Badassery Time.

Saying yes . . . saying yes is courage.

Saying yes is the sun.

Saying yes is life.

11

Yes to No, Yes to Difficult Conversations

When I was fifteen, I took my first driver's ed class.

I was excited. I had studied the rules of the road; I had my permit neatly folded in my genuine faux leather Duran Duran wallet. I was all about getting my license because once I did, my dad was going to let me drive myself to school in the butter-colored Renault Alliance that was in our driveway. Driving meant freedom. Driving meant that one day, one day so, so soon, I could drive right out of suburbia and drive right into someplace I was meant to be. Like Paris.

(Do not interject with your "Don't you know you'd drive into the ocean, you moron?" stuff right now. You're ruining the moment. This was my first driving lesson. All my dreams were coming true. Let me have this one.)

That afternoon my mom dropped me off at the public school where driver's ed was offered. I waited patiently for my instructor to arrive and when he did, I got to climb behind the wheel of a car for the very first time.

It was awesome. Totally. Totally.

Butterflies zipping around my stomach, I looked at the instructor. Patient and kind, a little balding, he was known as a nice man. He smiled at me, reassuring. I smiled back and asked what he wanted me to do.

That is pretty much the last thing I remember.

Turns out that what he wanted me to do was start the car and drive out of the parking lot, down the road, up the ramp and right out onto the freeway.

The *freeway*.

Much later, while he was pressing a wet paper towel to my tearstained face and explaining to me why I didn't need to ever tell this story to my mother (my mother who makes Khaleesi and her dragons look like Winnie the Pooh and would have removed his limbs), I learned the instructor had gotten his schedule mixed up. He had mistakenly thought I was another, more experienced student.

Just before my mom arrived, I asked him what had happened.

"Did I hit anything?"

The phrase *blood drained from his face* is real, y'all. I saw it happen to the instructor. That's the first time I realized that I had been scared literally out of my mind.

That is the first time my brain was wiped clean by fear.

That was the first painting removed from my wall.

And when I look back on it now, all I can think is . . .

. . . why did I let that happen?

When the driver's ed instructor told me to turn onto the ramp that led to the freeway, why didn't I put my foot on the brake and put the car in Park and look at him and say that one word that would have changed everything? That one word that might have kept the paintings from ever being at risk?

One. Word.

NO.

No is a powerful word. To me, it's the single most powerful word in the English language. Said clearly, strongly and with enough frequency and force, it can alter the course of history.

Want an example?

Rosa Parks.

Let's butterfly-wing Rosa Parks.

What if Rosa Parks doesn't say no? What if Rosa Parks says *Yeah, okay, fine, dangit, I'll give up my seat and move to the back of this bus*? The Montgomery Bus Boycott does not have its exact perfect hero—a lovely, genteel lady, kind and firm, a lady who captures the imagination and conscience of America—and maybe never happens.

My father's people are from Alabama. As are some of my mother's. If the bus boycott doesn't happen, does it alter the course of their lives? Do they never meet in Chicago? Am I never born? Would I be sitting in my house writing this in Los Angeles, California, today?

Why, hello, narcissism. It has been pages and pages since we've seen each other. How you must have missed me.

Yes. Yes, I just suggested that Rosa Parks's saying no on that bus is about me. Did you think I wouldn't find a way to bring everything right back to me?

If I can't make an entire civil rights movement about myself, well . . . what is the point of being a self-centered American? Did I tell you that *you* had to make Rosa Parks's amazing sacrifice about *you*?

No.

No, I did not.

NO.

Most powerful word in the English language.

See, you were trying to tell me about my ridiculous self and I just shut you down.

With NO.

Roll with me, friends.

Want another example?

When I was making the pilot for *Grey's Anatomy*, we were lucky enough to work with a seriously brilliant casting director named Linda Lowy. Linda, who by the way is one of my favorite people, has a way of just knowing when an actor will be the key that fits the lock that turns the story in my brain. Linda and her partner, John, have put together every cast of every show I've ever done. Now we have a shorthand. I'll call her up.

"Linda," I'll say, "I need a man."

Linda, who is refined and elegant, does not say the thing my friend Gordon would say, which is "Everybody needs a man but you especially need one. Look how tightly you are wound. Get your client to a meeting now!"

Linda probes a bit to find out what *kind* of man I'm looking to cast and for what and then she hangs up the phone and a week or so later, she'll be on the phone telling me that she has found me a man.

And that man will be Jeffrey Dean Morgan. Or Eric Dane. Or Jesse Williams. Or . . . I could keep going forever.

When I met Linda, I was new to TV. I was new to casting. Heck, I was new to removing my pajamas during the workday and leaving the house—up until the pilot of *Grey's Anatomy*, I'd been a movie writer working at home. It was all new to me. And I was so darn happy to be in shiny TV world—wide-eyed and corn-fed and bubbly about it all. Everyone was showing me the ropes and I was just along for the ride.

There was a moment in the *Grey's* casting process before we'd even laid eyes on Sandra Oh when everyone was pushing me to cast some actor as Cristina whom they all thought was great. I honestly can't remember who the actor was but Betsy thought she was great, the studio thought she was great, everyone thought she was great. And she was great. I, too, thought she was great. But I did not want to cast her. Now I know what I did not know then—at this level, everyone is a great actor; there are no bad actors, there are just actors who do not fit your vision. This actor was just . . . not the key that fit the lock that turned the story in my brain. But at the time, I didn't know that was the problem. At the time, I just didn't want to cast her.

Everyone was pushing. Betsy was pushing. The studio was pushing. I was dodging phone calls. I was saying vague things. I was telling people that I needed to think.

These were the very early days, before we'd even shot a single frame of footage. I was incredibly excited but the introvert in me was regretting being at the epicenter of a production. Everyone kept asking me what I wanted to do. In those early days, I was scared to have an opinion because I was afraid of having a different opinion than everyone else.

Betsy kept staring at me, bewildered. Who in the hell had replaced Shonda with a weird pod person? Because the Shonda she had known during the writing process had been enthusiastic and opinionated. Now I seemed to be fading. I kept my head down and avoided looking at her.

One morning, Linda called me at home. I'd only known her a matter of weeks and at this point, I'm fairly sure she thought I was a moron who did not know how to speak because I only mumbled to say things like "More cookies," "I don't know" and "I need to go write more" before escaping the room.

Linda got me on the phone.

"Shonda," she said firmly, "you are wasting time. You are wasting resources. Actors are being snapped up by other shows every other minute. We are at a standstill because you will not say what you want. You and I both know you do not want to cast this actor. So you need to say so—so we can move on and cast someone you do want. This is your show and if you cast someone you do not want, it will not be your show. You need to tell everyone no."

We got everyone else on the phone. As everyone poured out their reasons for why this actor was going to be the perfect Cristina, I could feel Linda breathing on the line. She was waiting for me to speak up. *If I say no, they could decide I don't know what I'm doing and take this whole thing away from me,* I worried. *If I say no, they could just do what they want anyway.*

Finally, I blurted out, "No."

Silence.

I had never asserted myself before. There was a pause.

Betsy tried to reason with me. To her, I'm sure I sounded a bit crazy. I'd been so busy mumbling and being along for the ride that I'd never said a word. As far as she knew I loved the actor.

"But, Shonda—"

"No. I do not want her. I do not want to write for her. No. No. NO."

There was a pause. Then I heard Betsy's voice rev up. Now I can tell you that energy comes from excitement. There is nothing Betsy loves more as a producer than someone who actually has a creative vision and isn't afraid to fight for it.

"Okay," she said. "No on that chick. Okay!"

I could also feel her relief. Shonda had returned.

I was just as relieved. That was my very first no at work. My first moment of asserting myself as the leader, the captain of what we all thought was going to be a tiny sailboat called *Untitled Shonda Rhimes Pilot* but turned out to be a gigantic ocean liner called *Grey's Anatomy*.

My first NO.

And my favorite NO.

Because of that NO? I decided that I was steering the ship. And I started behaving that way. I started behaving like the thing in my brain was our only true north. And that we would be guided by it no matter what.

Because of that NO?

Sandra Oh walked in the door the very next day. The lock in my brain found its key. Cristina Yang was born.

yesyesyesyesyesyesyesyesyesyesyesyesyesyesyesyes

No is powerful. It's a big weapon to have in your arsenal. But it is a very tough weapon to deploy.

Everyone knows how difficult it is to say no.

It's one of the reasons why people seem to be comfortable asking you for favors they have no business asking you for. They know how hard it is to say no.

"Can you watch my kids for an hour?"

"Can I wear your diamond earrings?"

"Can I borrow your car?"

Or telling you to do things they have no business telling you to do.

"I am gonna need you to work my shift."

"I need you to loan me a hundred dollars."

Now, the answer to all of these should be no—unless the person coming to me is one of my closest friends or a member of my immediate family. Frankly, if they aren't your closest friends or family, they have no business even asking the question. No. No. No.

But it's hard to say no.

Even though I've become a master at saying no at work, it's different in my personal life. Everything is different in your personal life. At work I have the shield of speaking on behalf of what is best for the story, the show, the cast, the crew, the staff. Outside of work, I'm speaking on behalf of what is best for me.

And who am I?

I'm great at taking care of other people. So why am I so bad at taking care of myself? Why am I so unwilling to show myself the same kindness and consideration, to cut myself the same slack, to give myself the same protection and care that I would give anyone else?

This problem did not change as I got more successful at work.

It got worse.

This Year of Yes continuously revealed new things to me as I shed layers of myself. When I got to this yes, this desire not to be a doormat, the Yes to saying No, the television upfronts—the industry's yearly New York presentation of each network's new fall shows to advertisers—had just happened. I'd just stood onstage at Lincoln Center with Viola Davis at my side as ABC announced to the world that the most valuable piece of real estate in television was going to be mine. They were programming Thursday night with Shondaland shows. Not just a piece of it. All of it. *Grey's Anatomy* at eight, *Scandal* at nine and *How to Get Away with Murder* at ten.

Thirteen years ago, when I told my agent, Chris, that I wanted to switch from writing movies to TV, I jokingly said "I want to take over the world through television." I jokingly said it a lot—to friends, to my sisters, to everyone.

What's your goal?

I want to take over the world through television.

I said it jokingly. But I was not joking. I was never joking.

And now it was happening. Onstage at Lincoln Center with Viola Davis standing beside me.

My dream was coming true.

You know what happens when all of your dreams come true?

Nothing.

I realized a very simple truth: that success, fame, having all my dreams come true would not fix or improve me, it wasn't an instant potion for personal growth. Having all my dreams come true only seemed to magnify whatever qualities I already possessed.

So my inability to be a shark? To Pope someone? To fix, to handle?

To say no?

Still powerfully in place at work on behalf of my shows and my people. In Shondaland, I truly was a gladiator. I was fearless. I battled with endless energy.

But outside the office? On my own behalf?

Somehow I am back in the pantry again.

Let me know if you need any canned goods.

I was like a helpless baby lamb waiting to be slaughtered.

A grown-ass television-show-running helpless baby lamb.

The craziest thing about becoming successful is that all kinds of people decide that you are rich. And not just rich. They decide you are a bank. Now, the truth is, nobody *actually* knows your situation and the assumption that you have a ton of money is just that—an assumption. And not always a true one.

If I were truly rich—I mean really actually money-for-several-generations wealthy—I would be in Vermont. Making jam. And writing novels. While my muscular handyman boyfriend who would be named Fitz or Derek or Jake or Burke chopped wood and grilled dinner.

You see I'm not in Vermont, right? You see I'm not making jam? And that the only Fitzes and Dereks are fictional?

You see that because you are here hanging out with me. But others . . . they get those cartoon dollar signs inside their cartoon eyeballs.

The moment I had a TV show on the air, people came out of the woodwork. People I knew, people I hadn't talked to in years, people I only vaguely knew, people who maybe knew someone who might have known my mom, people who were related to me by the thinnest of threads . . .

Jobs, places to stay, money, scripts to be read, a part on the show, audition opportunities, tuition, films to be financed, introductions to celebrities, investments in their companies, a meeting with the child of their friend—you name it and I've been asked for it.

At first I couldn't believe it. I really couldn't.

I also couldn't say no.

I would try. And then I'd find myself nervously babbling some excuse and talking myself into a circle that somehow always ended in my saying yes.

My mother would stare at me in disbelief. Outraged on my behalf.

"*Who* called you and asked for *what*? Do we know these people? Give me their number and I will take care of this."

A NO conversation was a five-brownie emergency. At the rate I was getting requests, I was going to need to be fork-lifted to a special facility in a very short time. Do not laugh. Being forklifted is not a joke—it's my dark place.

But then, fortunately, as suddenly as the deluge of requests started coming in, they started to slow to a trickle. Years later, I learned my sister Sandie became an expert at stepping in and deflecting crazy requests for favors before I even knew of them.

I have good sisters.

Gordon, Zola and Scottie told me they dealt with it as well. My parents got inundated. Everyone around me did. And they willingly acted as human shields. Forcing back the herds of weirdos and audacious money seekers.

But they couldn't force back the people I thought were friends. People I considered myself close to. People I was naive enough to date. The foxes in my henhouse.

Soon after the Year of Yes began, someone I know well and love a lot (I'm going to randomly call this person . . . Laura) asked me to give her a large amount of money. A very large amount of money. More money than I would ever considering spending at one time. Laura just casually asked for this sum of money as if she was asking me for five dollars.

I am from the Midwest. I will fight you if you try to tell me to buy a fancy cheese—bulk cheese never hurt anybody. And so what if cheap toilet paper is scratchy? The scratchy is how you know you are clean.

You see my point?

I am not going to feel good parting with that kind of money.

Gordon, Scott and Zola and I have dinner.

"Say yes to saying no," they tell me. "Nobody should be asking you for that kind of money. That is your money. You earned that money. You worked for that money. You don't owe it to anyone. I don't care if you were a zillionaire, you are not obligated to give anyone a dime of your money."

"*No* is a complete sentence," Sandie lectures me. "You say no and you say good-bye. You don't owe anyone an explanation."

No is a complete sentence.

I've heard that cliché over and over.

So, I decide to treat saying no in the same way I treat saying thank you. Say no and then don't say anything else.

I come up with three different clear ways of saying no.

- "I am going to be unable to do that."
- Zola gives me: "That is not going to work for me."
- And there's simply: "No."

I write the lines down on a Post-it. Then I slap the Post-it on the front of my computer monitor so that it sticks out from the side like a flag. I stare at it as I get on the phone with Laura. Laura, a person I have considered a friend for years. My hands are shaking. My mind goes blank. I have to stare at the script on the Post-it in order to say the words.

"About the money," I say softly, "I am going to be unable to do that."

The rant sent in my direction because I will not hand over my money is stunning. As I listen—and I do sit and listen—I feel a tremendous sense of relief wash over me.

And in that moment, I am set free.

The reason I've been so afraid to say no is clear. I worried, "What if she gets angry? What if she doesn't want to be friends anymore? What if she yells and things turn ugly?"

Now it's happening. And all I can think is, "Good. Now I know." The worst thing that could happen is happening and . . . so what? It isn't so awful. I'm happier knowing what kind of person this really is than I was not knowing. Saying no, what I *really* wanted to say, allowed Laura to reveal herself by getting her to say what she really wanted to say. And what she wanted to say was she was using me for what I could do for her. That she resented me. That I was her ATM machine.

And you know what I say to that?

Aw. Hell. No.

Laura pauses in her rant. "This," I think, "is the part where I am supposed to apologize and offer to give her the money."

Later, Zola will tell me that while I may not see it, six months earlier I would have apologized and handed over the money to avoid any and all drama, pain and conflict. Zola will gently imply that I used to be a doormat.

But right now, I can hear my old friend Laura breathing on the phone. And I calmly fill the silence.

"This? Isn't gonna work for me. No. Bye."

Bye, Felicia.

And I hang up.

I literally run around the room. I do that sometimes. When I get overly excited, I run around the room. I did it during the Red Wedding scene of *Game of Thrones*. I did it when they picked up the pilot for *Grey's Anatomy* to series. I did it the moment I got the call Harper was about to be born.

I feel fantastic. I am on a high for days. I tell the story to anyone who will listen. People keep trying to comfort me over the loss of a friend.

But they don't get it. I did not lose a friend. I gained a second superpower.

I can make stuff up. And I can say no.

Wait.

I can do *more* than say no.

I can say *anything*.

I can make stuff up. And I can say *anything*.

I can say *anything* to *anyone*.

Any difficult conversation, any tough issue I have sitting in the pit of my stomach, any unsaid confessions, any itchy little resentment and unpleasant business?

I can talk about it.

I *want* to talk about it.

Because no matter how hard a conversation is, I know that on the other side of that difficult conversation lies peace. Knowledge. An answer is delivered. Character is revealed. Truces are formed. Misunderstandings are resolved.

Freedom lies across the field of the difficult conversation.

And the more difficult the conversation, the greater the freedom.

When someone says something petty or nasty, one of those little passive-aggressive things that would usually just pick at me for days, my new response is not to shut the door and bitch to anyone who will listen. Now? The moment they say it?

"What did you mean by that?" I ask in a calm voice.

It startles them. I realize that most of us aren't used to being spoken TO. We are used to being spoken about. We are used to avoiding all the conflict. And of course, in the avoidance all we're doing is creating more drama.

A good friend was the queen of mumbling under her breath.

"Well, too bad for you," she'd mumble when I told her about something minor that had made for a difficult day at work.

"What did you mean by that?"

She looked up.

"What?"

" 'Well, too bad for you.' That's what you said. What did you mean by that?"

She was mortified. She hadn't been aware that anyone else could hear her mumblings. She didn't know that her inner monologue of bitterness was audible to the world. Her apology was sincere; the work she has to do on herself is her own.

When something wasn't going well, when there was a conflict or someone was upset or being difficult, the more introverted me would flee and hope it all went away. The new me wades right into the deep end and asks, "What's wrong?"

yesyesyesyesyesyesyesyesyesyesyesyesyesyesyesyes

It has been unexpectedly glorious so far. Simply being willing to have the conversations acted as a sort of magical spell. Some potion was tossed into the ether of the universe. Because the moment I said yes to the challenge, the moment I was open to having the conversations, suddenly in that instant my life was changed.

I grew more courageous; I shed some shyness, some awkwardness, some social fear. Each time I said yes, I gained new friends and new experiences and found myself getting involved with projects that I never would have dreamed I could be part of.

I laughed more. I was bolder. I was brazen. I spoke my mind and spoke it loud. And as busy as I was, I felt like I had more free time than ever; I realized I'd been wasting a huge amount of time and energy on complaining and feeling sorry for myself, being dark and twisty me. Now I wasn't interested in being that person. Not when it was so much easier to just open my mouth and talk.

yesyesyesyesyesyesyesyesyesyesyesyesyesyesyesyesyes

I've become kind of obsessed with difficult conversations. Mostly because of how calm life is when you are willing to have them. Also because of how much easier it is not to eat the cake when I'm not stressed out or holding a grudge or full of hurt feelings.

I stuck a Post-it on my bathroom mirror that says, "I can say it or I can eat it." As corny as it sounds, it's true. I wish I'd learned to say yes twenty-five years ago. Between dieting and never saying what I thought, I wasted a lot of time.

But I was making up for it. The yeses were adding up. The swagger, the play, the thank-yous, the difficult conversations, the weight loss—I was beginning to seem like a different person.

Over one of our weekly dinners, my three closest friends informed me of this.

"You don't look the same, act the same or even feel like the same person," Zola told me.

Scott and Gordon agreed.

"You are strutting," Scott said. "You glow now."

"You used to be all slumped over," Gordon said. "Depressed and 'don't look at me.' That girl is gone."

Gone. Girl.

yesyesyesyesyesyesyesyesyesyesyesyesyesyesyesyes

Saying what you think and wading into the deep end don't always have a happy ending. Difficult conversations are something of a gamble and you have to be willing to be okay with the outcome. And you have to know, going in, where you draw the line.

You have to know *when* in the conversation you are going to say no.

You have to know when you are going to say, "That doesn't work for me."

You have to know when to say, "I'm done."

You have to know when to say, "This isn't worth it."

"*You* aren't worth it."

The more I said what I thought, the more I was willing to dive into the difficult conversations, the more I was willing to say yes to *me*, the less I was willing to allow people in my life who left me emptier and unhappier and more insecure than before I saw them.

My friend who asked for all the money isn't the last person I walked away from during this Year of Yes.

No. No that friend was not.

No.

12

Yes to People

When Chris #1 told me that I was going to be presented with the Ally for Equality Award by the Human Rights Campaign, I was immediately more worried about my dress than I was about my speech. Giving speeches didn't even give me a twinge these days. I cared about what I was going to say, of course. But I was no longer afraid to say it.

I was rounding the corner into what felt like the final lap of my *Yes* run. It was starting to feel simple. I had the hang of it, this *Yes* thing. I owned it. I was smug and self-righteous about it. Oh, arrogance, *there* you are . . .

I just felt like I had the whole thing under control. I was running like a gazelle toward that finish line.

And then like any long race, that final lap got hard. I hit

a wall. Turns out the beginning had been easy. The toughest part was yet to come.

I was still struggling with how to speak up for myself. How to stand up for myself. How to gladiate for myself. It was ironic.

I knew a large part of the reason I was getting this award was because by portraying LGBTQ characters on TV, I was speaking up, standing up, gladiating for others. And I couldn't do it for myself.

Shedding weight was one thing.

Shedding people was quite another.

I had just shed a friend. A close one.

I had never felt more alone.

I was fighting the desire to take to my bed with *Doctor Who* and a box of Thin Mints. I wanted a little veal practice. For the first time in a long, long time, I wanted to be numb.

When it was time to try on gowns for the event, Dana stood over me as I curled up in a ball on my sofa.

"I don't think I can do it. I'm sick. I'm dying."

Dana didn't say anything. Not a word. She stood there a moment and then, just when I began to wonder if Chris #1 was now hosting How to Make Shonda Move Her Ass Seminars, she turned away.

And began unpacking gowns. Stunningly beautiful evening gowns.

No need for a seminar. Turns out that is How to Make Shonda Move Her Ass.

Later that week, the dress hangs on the closet door. Sandie stands at the foot of my bed. I'm trying to remember how veal practice works. I tell her I cannot go to this event. I feel too alone. She tells me that I *will* go. She tells me that she will go with me. And then she tells me to invite more people. Invite *your* people. *Gather your people.*

"A*lone*," she snorts and shakes her head at my foolishness. As if being alone was ever an option.

The morning of the HRC gala, I write my speech. That evening I feel vulnerable standing there on that stage. I feel like I've ripped a page from my diary and am reading it aloud. And yet, it is exactly what I want to say. I want to give everyone what Sandie gave me. The snort, the head shake, *gather your people.*

Here it is:

HUMAN RIGHTS CAMPAIGN SPEECH
Delivered March 14, 2015
Los Angeles, California

YOU ARE NOT ALONE

I have been a writer since before I could spell.

I used to dictate stories into a tape recorder with my sister Sandie. Then I tried to get my mother to type them up. I was maybe three. And when I learned to spell . . . writing opened *worlds.*

The six of us on one of our mother's flawless Thanksgivings. See that extremely perfect, amazing baby? That's me. Delorse is the one working the beehive updo. From left to right: James, Delorse, Elnora, Shonda, Tony, Sandie (seated)

A happy childhood in the rainbow multicultural suburbs of the 1970s. This is right before the time I discovered the magic of the pantry. That awesome hot pants–jumpsuit that I'm working? Delorse sewed it.

There's a book hidden in the back of my underpants in this photo. For real. I'm going to find a place to hide and read as soon as this photo is over.

The glasses. The blouse. The hairdo. Let's all agree not to talk about my style choices, okay? Oh: there's a book hidden down the back of my pants in this photo too.

5

That nerd is me graduating from 8th grade and heading to high school. That nerdy joy you see on my face is academic excitement. Also band geek excitement. I'm planning to rock my oboe in high school!

Sandie, my parents, Delorse and I headed off to the Emmy
Awards in 2006. Look closely: see how young everyone
looks? A lot of Benjamin Buttoning going on . . .

Delorse and her Thanksgiving turkey!

That was the most fun I could have
while worrying about fear-snot. Jimmy
Kimmel was incredibly nice. That big vase
of flowers came from Jimmy after.

11

Marc Cherry saving
me at TCAs.

12 Chris DiIorio.

13

14

My own Dartmouth
graduation day in 1991.

15

The view from that podium
is intimidating. But truly,
I've never had so much fun.

16

Beckett, Emerson and Harper: they make my world spin.

Jenny McCarthy.

21

The more I work the
larger I get. . . .

22

23

Every year we have our photo taken at family camp. Before and after have never been so obvious. Mostly? It's my smile.

I am here to speak at the *Hollywood Reporter*'s
Women in Entertainment event.

The Mindy Project! And me! That happened!
(Ed Weeks, Adam Pally, me and Ike Barinholtz)

Speaking at the HRC gala.

My friends joined me for the HRC gala: my sister Sandie, Donnie White, Scott Brown, me, Matthew Perrye and Gordon James (plus Zola, who'd just rushed home to her babysitter). I have found my tribe.

All those years of marriage and my parents are still MFEO.

The Ride or Dies: Gordon James, Zola Mashariki and
Scott Brown on one of our many trips.

31 Sandra Oh and Kevin McKidd just after Sandra's final table read.

32

Sandra Oh and Isaiah Washington rehearse the Chocolate Factory scene.

33

Sandra Oh, Justin Chambers and me right before Sandra's final table read.

Cristina hangs on to a slippery fish and tries to regain what she's lost.

Meredith and Cristina dance it out for the very last time.

Full circle moment: back at TCAs but having a good time!

Definitely enjoying it all more.

Yes, yes, yes.

Nothing else provides that singular hum in my brain, that special trip to the imagination. Writing was . . . well, for me it was like sitting down at a piano for the first time and realizing that I always knew how to play. Writing was my melody. Writing was who I was. Writing was ME.

I spent my school days writing in journals. I still have them. Little fabric-covered books, frayed and fading. They're boxed up in my attic—about twenty of them, I think.

Little books filled with hopes and dreams and stories and pain.

Let me describe myself as a kid: highly intelligent, way too chubby, incredibly sensitive, nerdy and painfully shy. I wore Coke-bottle-thick glasses. Two cornrow braids traveled down the sides of my skull in a way that was just not pretty on me. And here's the kicker—I was often the only black girl in my class.

I did not have friends.

No one is meaner than a pack of human beings faced with someone who is different.

I was very much alone.

So . . .

I wrote.

I created friends. I named them and wrote every detail about them. I gave them stories and homes and families. I wrote about their parties and their dates and their friendships and their lives and they were so very real to me that—

You see, Shondaland, the imaginary land of Shonda, has existed since I was eleven years old.

I built it in my mind as a place to hold my stories. A safe place. A space for my characters to exist. A space for ME to exist. Until I could get the hell out of being a teenager and could run out into the world and be myself.

Less isolated, less marginalized, less invisible in the eyes of my peers.

Until I could find my people in the real world.

I don't know if anyone has noticed but I only ever write about one thing: being alone. The fear of being alone, the desire to not be alone, the attempts we make to find our person, to keep our person, to convince our person to not leave us alone, the joy of being with our person and thus no longer alone, the devastation of being left alone.

The need to hear the words: *You are not alone.*

The fundamental human need for one human being to hear another human being say to them: "You are not alone. You are seen. I am with you. You are not alone."

I get asked a lot by reporters and tweeters why I am so invested in "diversity" on television. "Why is it so important to have diversity on TV?" they say. "Why is it so challenging to have diversity?" "Why does Cyrus need to be gay?"

I really hate the word *diversity*. It suggests something . . . other. As if it is something . . . special. Or rare.

Diversity!

As if there is something unusual about telling stories involving women and people of color and LGBTQ characters on TV.

I have a different word: *NORMALIZING.*

I'm normalizing TV.

I am making TV look like the world looks. Women, people of color, LGBTQ people equal WAY more than 50 percent of the population. Which means it ain't out of the ordinary. I am making the world of television look NORMAL.

I am NORMALIZING television.

You should get to turn on the TV and see your tribe. And your tribe can be any kind of person, anyone you identify with, anyone who feels like you, who feels like home, who feels like truth. You should get to turn on the TV and see your tribe, see your people, someone like you out there, existing. So that you know on your darkest day that when you run (metaphorically or physically RUN), there is somewhere, someone, to run TO. Your tribe is waiting for you.

You are not alone.

The goal is that everyone should get to turn on the TV and see someone who looks like them and loves like them. And just as important, everyone should turn on the TV and see someone who **doesn't** look like them and love like them. Because perhaps then they will learn from them.

Perhaps then they will not isolate them.

Marginalize them.

Erase them.

Perhaps they will even come to recognize themselves in them.

Perhaps they will even learn to love them.

I think that when you turn on the television and you see love, from anyone, with anyone, to anyone—*real love*—a service has been done for you. Your heart has somehow been expanded, your mind has somehow grown. Your soul has been opened a little more. You've experienced something.

The very idea that love exists, that it is possible, that one can have a "person". . .

You are not alone.

Hate diminishes, love expands.

I do a lot of talking in my writers' rooms about how images matter. The images you see on television matter. They tell you about the world. They tell you who you are. What the world is like. They shape you. We all know this. There have been studies.

So if you never see a Cyrus Beene on TV, ever? An older, badass, take-no-prisoners, Republican, conservative, Rumsfeldian gay man who loved his husband, James, so deeply and tried desperately not to kill him . . .

If you never see James dragging Cyrus into the twenty-first century . . .

If you never see young Connor Walsh on *How to Get Away with Murder* getting to have the same kind of slutty dating life we've seen straight characters have on TV season after season after season . . .

If you never see Erica Hahn exuberantly give what's become known as the Leaves on Trees monologue telling Callie that she's realized she is a lesbian . . .

If you never see openly bisexual Callie Torres stare her father down and holler (my favorite line ever), "You can't pray away the gay!!!" at him . . .

If you never see a transgender character on TV have family, understanding, a Dr. Bailey to love and support her . . .

If you never see any of those people on TV . . .

What do you learn about your importance in the fabric of society? What do straight people learn? What does that tell young people? Where does that leave them? Where does that leave any of us?

I get letters and tweets and people coming up to me on the street. Telling me so many incredible stories. The dad telling me about how something he saw on one of my shows gave him a way to understand his son when he came out. Or the teenagers, all the *teenagers*, man, who tell me they learned the language to talk to their parents about being gay or lesbian. The teenage girls who have found a community of peers and support online because of the Callie-Arizona relationship—Calzona.

I get story after story.

There were times in my youth when writing those stories

in Shondaland quite literally saved my life. And now I get kids telling me it quite literally saves theirs. That is beyond humbling.

And every single time it comes down to one thing.

You are not alone.

Nobody should be alone.

So.

I write.

We are only on the edge of change. There is still so much more work to be done. I'm going to accept this award as encouragement and not as accomplishment. I don't think the job is finished yet. I have a lot of lesbian and gay friends whose marriages I would like to see recognized in every single state in this country.★

And there are so many minds and laws that still need to be changed. I want to applaud the HRC for their work in fighting so hard for equality and the end of discrimination of all kinds for the LGBT community. The work you are doing is tremendous.

Writing is no different for me now than it was when I was talking into that tape recorder with my sister Sandie.

Yes, it's on a larger landscape.

★On June 26, 2015, the United States Supreme Court legalized same sex marriage in all fifty states (high five, America!), and so this part of my speech is now thankfully out of date.

Yes, it's all of Thursday night.

Yes, I am less shy, arguably less nerdy, clearly better styled. The glasses have been replaced by contacts.

I am still often the only black girl in my class. (Look around you.)

But here's the thing: I am no longer alone.

The characters that lived inside my head are on the television screen. They are not just my friends now—they are also everyone else's. Shondaland is open, and if I am doing my job right, there will be a person here for everyone.

I want to say how much I appreciate all of the support and kindness I have received. A lot of people out there have been quick to come to my defense in wonderful ways. Especially after I tweet angry. I'm very proud of what I said to the person who tweeted me the nasty comment about "gay scenes." I would say *Bye, Felicia* again and again. But sometimes I wish I thought first and tweeted later—because think of what an even more awesome thing I COULD have said with a re-write and some notes?!

But seriously, still, I am eternally grateful.

Finally I want to say this:

If you are a kid and you are out there and you are chubby and not so cute and nerdy and shy and invisible and in pain, whatever your race, whatever your gender, whatever your sexual orientation, I'm standing here to tell you: you are not alone.

Your tribe of people, they are out there in the world. Waiting for you.

How do I know this for sure?

Because mine?

Are sitting at that table right over *there*.

Thank you.

13

Yes to Dancing It Out
(with the right people)

I'm sitting in the editing room at Prospect Studios with my editor Joe Mitacek. We're fighting over what song to use. This debate has raged on for weeks. It's the Season Ten finale of *Grey's Anatomy*. The scene is iconic: Meredith and Cristina are dancing it out in an on-call room for the very last time. The song that will play as we watch them dance has epic meaning for me and for the fans who have watched these characters grow from interns to attendings, cautious young women to powerhouses. We have been with them for more than two hundred episodes at this point. More than a decade of our lives and theirs. This is the very last time anyone will see Cristina Yang on-screen. The scene, the song, the edit—everything has to be right.

When the scene was initially filmed, a fast, awesome hip-hop dance song was used to rev the actors up and give them energy. Now, in the editing room, there are opinions coming in from all sides. Everyone who was there during filming believes that anything other than a fast dance song is going to make Sandra and Ellen look bad dancing.

I find this to be ridiculous.

I don't believe either Sandra or Ellen has *ever* looked bad dancing in her life. It's not possible. Sandra has a rock-star cool rhythm-nation thing happening and Ellen's got bounce, somehow both luminous and everything gangsta at all times. That the two of them can shake it with such distinct individuality and yet still convey so much kinship and harmony is what inspired the entire concept of dancing it out in the first place.

They've been doing it for ten seasons.

This ain't no trick of editing, people.

These women can *move*.

I was not there during filming—I am *never there during filming* (well, almost never) because I can't be in five places at once. This time I wasn't there because I was at my daughter's school. I missed the live performance. So I haven't been pre-influenced.

And anyway I don't care.

I don't want a fast song.

A fast song feels wrong.

A fast song bugs me.

A fast song is all . . .

Joe wants to know why I don't like it.

It's a reasonable question.

Except I can't answer it.

I don't have a way of explaining why I don't like it.

I don't know *why*.

I just don't like it.

It makes me prickly in my true-north-y creases.

We argue. We debate. We fight.

These are not useless exercises. I want my editors to fight with me. I like to be challenged. I like to be proven wrong.

I am deeply suspicious of instant agreement.

Instant agreement terrifies me.

Joe has been working here in post-production for almost the entire lifetime of the show. He's gone from assistant editor to lead editor in his time here. He's been around the block. He knows how these editing debates go. He knows he has a shot at prevailing if he can get me to stare at the story from a different angle, a different perspective. If he can tilt the landscape just a little bit . . .

So we battle it out.

yes *yes* yes *yes* yes *yes* yes *yes* yes *yes* yes *yes* yes *yes* yes *yes*

Once I said Yes to difficult conversations, once I said Yes to saying No, I made an interesting discovery. That discovery was: happy, whole people are drawn to happy, whole people, but nothing makes a toxic person more miserable and destructive than a happy, whole person. Unhappy people do not like it when a fellow unhappy person becomes happy.

I am absolutely sure that this is true.

Because I used to be an unhappy person.

And nothing was more frustrating than seeing a fellow bitter, jaded, toxic, dark and twisty friend find their way up into the sun. Like a vampire trying to save one of its own, you want to drag them back into the dark. And you truly think you are doing the right thing. I was clinging to the dark and twisty misery. It was what I knew. And I needed it. I needed it the same way I needed the fatness. It was easier than trying. Being dark and twisty gave me permission to not want anything more than the miserable status quo. To never hope, to never be optimistic. Dark and twisty takes up the time and space in my head. It's a hall pass: I don't have to do anything about my problems if I am busy complaining and feeling sorry for myself.

Now I was the one standing on the mountaintop with a clear, sunny view. And I could see there was no room for twisty up here.

yesyesyesyesyesyesyesyesyesyesyesyesyesyesyesyes

Before the Year of Yes, if you had asked me who my close friends were, I would have confidently rattled off a list of names of people I love, people I have known for years and years. The people for whom I would do anything.

My *people*. My *posse*. My *tribe*.

My Bonnies and my Clydes.

My Ride or Die list.

A Ride or Die list is no joke.

I mean, I've never ridden or died and I am a middle-class girl who used to hang out in the pantry in the suburbs where the only Bonnie I had ever heard of was Bonne Bell lip gloss, but, you know . . .

My Ride or Die list before the Year of Yes was very specific. Definite. I can say the names in my sleep.

As I write this book about the Year of Yes?

That Ride or Die list? What does it look like?

It is the exact same list. The exact same names. No subtractions. It's just that not everyone on the list . . .

. . . exists.

Well, everyone *exists*.

It's just that not all of them are real.

For the last eleven years, there has been one name on my Ride or Die list who only exists inside the walls of Seattle Grace Mercy West/Grey Sloan Memorial Hospital. I'm not insane. I know she isn't real.

I just don't care.

Cristina Yang will always be one of my Ride or Dies.

*yes**yes***yes**yes**yes***yes**yes***yes**yes**yes***yes**yes**yes***yes**yes**yes*

People think the substance of a TV show is the words I've put on the paper. It's not. The substance of a show is character. And for me, characters may *begin* with the words I put on paper, but they are flat. Like empty balloons you pour out of a bag. The actor breathes the air into the words and suddenly what was flat is now fully three-dimensional and alive. More nuanced, funnier or sadder or more cruel or more vulnerable. I wrote and Sandra Oh breathed and what floated up was Cristina. OUR Cristina. The one Sandra and I made together.

That is who Cristina was. A piece of my soul and a piece of Sandra's soul wound around each other and placed on television. A human collaboration into imagination.

This Cristina that we made was a revelation. She was never silenced. Never small. Never too insecure to make good on her natural gifts. The Cristina of our collective dreams is larger than life and sure of her genius. And, as drawn by us, while often afraid, our Cristina was able to overcome her fears through sheer strength of will. She made bold choices. She felt fearless even when she was terrified.

It's no wonder I leaned into Cristina, wrote her more eloquently, colored her more brightly, drew outside her lines. Let her do and think and live in ways that voiced my dreams. She did not want to get married. She had a genius that she chased. She loved her work. I gave her a strident desire to not have children because while I adore children, I wanted to watch her fight that feminist battle and win. I wanted us to watch and admire a woman who did not want the things we have all been told we are supposed to want. I wanted us to befriend a woman who was busy throwing out the fairy tale and writing her own story. And with every portrait of her I finished, I allowed myself to pay a little less attention to my own fading gallery.

I receded into the background, where I could safely stand in Cristina's shadow. Where I could tiptoe in the footprints Cristina was imprinting alongside Meredith into the earth as they moved confidently across the landscape.

Cristina survived things in ways most characters wouldn't. She performed surgery with a gun pressed to her head. And she healed by catching a giant fish and holding it in her arms. During my darkest hours, my quietest saddest moments, my loneliest times, writing Cristina Yang fortified me.

That gun to her head and that fish in her arms? I wrote those stories for a reason. Those stories made me believe that all things were possible. Those stories were proof that I could survive anything, and Sandra's playing those moments out, breathing life into those words, into Cristina . . . Sandra's acting those words made my survival and resilience feel possible. Cristina Yang was the walking validation of my dreams.

As a nerdy introverted writer with an eye twitch who could barely speak up for herself? Let me tell you, dear friends, that was magic. And that kind of magic is crazy special.

The times Cristina and I had together were incredibly real to me. It sounds silly to say out loud. But it is true.

I have spent more time with Meredith and Cristina than many of my actual friends. Hours and hours in editing rooms, hours in writers' rooms, hours alone hovering over a script. When you watched TV, even by spending a full hour with Cristina once a week, you were likely spending more time with her than you spent with most people in your life.

That relationship was real.

That track I laid, that train?

It was real.

That train was speeding down those tracks, always on time, always a great ride.

But now, it is heading for its last stop.

We've almost reached the end of Cristina's line.

Sandra Oh is leaving the show. Soon she'll be gone. And when she goes, Cristina will go with her.

I am going to miss Cristina Yang.

I do not mean Sandra Oh. Of course, I'm going to miss Sandra. But I can see Sandra, I can talk to Sandra, I know where Sandra is.

No.

I mean that I am going to miss Cristina Yang so much that my heart hurts.

In the Year of Yes, this is one of the things that worries me the most. I'm not sure how I'm going to cope.

*yes*yes*yes*yes*yes*yes*yes*yes*yes*yes*yes*yes*yes*yes*yes*yes*yes*

Then something happens with one of the people on the Ride or Die list (let's call her . . . Pam?). Pam is a friend who I would describe as a genuinely wonderful person. Strong and really funny. Witty. Kind. Laid-back. Loyal. Adventurous. But as I leap into this challenging Year of Yes and take tentative steps toward being happy, Pam becomes a wall of ice. I find myself in situations more and more often where Pam seems angrier and angrier at me, her entire personality becomes more snide. There's a particularly ugly incident early on in the Year of Yes. Then a nasty argument happens months later. I spend a lot of time wondering if I've suddenly become overly sensitive or have somehow provoked this behavior. I find myself tentatively asking her about certain comments she makes or things she does that just feel plain mean to me. She runs from any conflict. I'm left baffled as to how my kind, confident friend has devolved this way. I'm concerned. But when it happens again, dramatic and passive-aggressive, I'm too far into the Yes life to put up with it. Now, all about throwing myself into difficult conversations, I confront her about what's going on. It does not go well.

I do what I always do when I want to talk something out, when I want to be told the unvarnished truth. I call on my inner circle Ride or Dies—Zola, Gordon and Scott. I know they'll tell me if I am at fault, if I've done something wrong that I am ignoring. We gather for dinner. I tell them everything. They are quiet, listening.

I keep waiting for one of them to jump in, to start some truth telling. To let me know what they think.

But nothing. They're glancing at one another. There's a silent debate going on with their eyebrows. But I'm not included.

"What?!" I am freaked out. The Ride or Dies *never* hold back. "Tell me."

Finally, one of them takes the plunge. "We've been wondering when this would happen. When you would finally notice how Pam was treating you."

What are they talking about?

They tell me they have always been suspicious of Pam. To their eyes, Pam is not happy that I am happy. She's suffering because I have changed, they have noticed. I am no longer willing to be a doormat, so Pam has no function. They very gently tell me *Pam has never been the person I thought she was.*

I have no words.

"Pam? *PAM?*" I am stunned. I am horrified. I am . . .

I sit very still for a moment. I close my eyes. And I think about everything I actually know about Pam. Everything I have actually seen or heard Pam do over the years I have known her. I can think of no examples of "strong" or "funny." She's always on edge—not laid-back. I've seen her be petty and vicious and full of gossip, so "loyal" is not quite the word. But . . . she was never like that for real? Right? *Right?*

I actually gasp out loud.

Because this is the first time I begin to understand something.

Those friends I created in my journals when I was eleven years old? The personalities and the backstories and the qualities I gave them? The stories I was spinning back then to create a world in which I had people? People who welcomed the chubby outsider with Coke-bottle-thick glasses and unfortunate braids? The characters I created so I would have a tribe?

I'm still doing it.

Right now.

I don't have any idea who Pam really is. Because every single quality that I have used in the past to describe her? Is just . . . track I've laid. Campfire.

I make stuff up for a living.

I made Pam up.

The role of Pam is being *played* by someone named Pam.

I have spent years having a totally fulfilling, completely awesome friendship with a person who is only a stand-in for a figment of my imagination.

I sit there. Realizing I am in a friendship in reality that mattered so little because I have created this friendship in my imagination that mattered so much to me. I don't even think I *like* the real Pam.

I don't even think I *know* Pam. She was just an . . .

"Avatar." Scott says it. "She was an avatar."

Yeah.

I am unsettled. I am even more unsettled when it happens with a second person on the list—let's call him . . . Ken? I could go into details on Ken but . . . second verse? Same as the first. That's the thing: there's no need to detail what happened with Ken because basically *it's exactly the same story.*

The Ride or Dies find this topic fascinating. We can't stop talking about it.

"Have I been just *rewriting* people's personalities to be better than the actual people? *Creating* them to serve whatever purpose I needed?" I gasp. "Oh my God, have I been putting *character* on top of it as well as food?"

That night, I can't sleep.

I'd been seeing what I want to see. And now, like with the food, now that I realize it, I no longer feel okay just slapping some storytelling over the reality of the people in my life.

It's not that I no longer feel okay.

I am no longer able to do it even if I wanted to.

Now that I see it, I can't unsee it. Everything is crystal clear. I've been left with Santa's stupid elves again. And I do not like Ill-fitting and Antsy. I don't want them in my house.

I feel sad. I'm grieving. I realize I'm not just losing Cristina. I'm losing Pam and Ken. Three fictional friends are going. Now that I can see the Shonda behind the curtain, now that I can see the track that has been laid, I can no longer see my Pam and my Ken. I just see these people who look like them wandering around the planet. My Pam and my Ken are dead. Truly dead. I can't get them back. The loss is painful.

At least I have a little more time with Cristina.

yesyesyesyesyesyesyesyesyesyesyesyesyesyesyesyes

Sandra and I have a deeply personal, strangely intertwined, intimate, cold, close, distant, vibrant relationship. The only kind of relationship possible for two people as emotional as we are, as mentally curious as we are and as creative as we are when we have spent ten years together as two halves of one person. We are like family. I see her and it is like no time has passed. We cry together, we laugh together, we tell each other dark secrets. We sit in restaurants and whisper to each other in a language that can only be translated in the context of this uniquely shared experience. It has been profound.

The fictional person Sandra and I made is beautiful and intimidating. Put Cristina up against any real person and there is no contest. No one else stands a chance. It's unfair and awful. And not at all a way to measure a real human being.

And yet. Who the hell cares?

She is the goal. She is freedom.

And that, of course, is *why* I created her. And I think why Sandra created her. For me, she was not just what I imagined. She was what I needed.

I am grateful to hear so many women tell me Cristina was what they needed too. I am not alone.

I once told someone that Cristina was one of my best friends. This person got a little upset.

"Cristina is America's best friend," she lectured. "You act like you have some kind of special thing."

I nod patiently.

"Yes, I know she's America's best friend. But I'm the one who gets to write what our best friend says and decide what she does and where she goes."

Wait, am I still in the pantry? I think so.

I make stuff up for a living. Yes.

But really, *I make stuff up for living.*

To live. To keep going.

My time with Cristina somehow saved me.

Cristina Yang raised her sword and chopped off the heads of every demon in my path. Making me feel safe. Protecting me. She was my test run for how each demon could be slayed. She ran every course first, she tried every weapon first, she attempted every tricky maneuver first.

She was an F.O.D. First. Only. Different.

And I ran behind her, getting all of her second chances.

She did that for me.

I now know that the demons out there are some version of me. I am aware that I am the only one chasing me, running me down, nipping at my heels. Trying to bite my head off. It's time to be a better friend to myself.

I'm not worried about my demons though. Cristina's getting off the train but she's leaving me her sword. I will chop the demon heads myself now.

I'm not afraid.

Cristina Yang made me brave.

Ride or Die.

I love a fictional character and I don't care who knows it.

She had been not only Meredith's person but also my own.

I laid this track.

I made this stuff up for living.

Here comes the train.

Let's dance it out. But first, we need to find a song . . .

yesyesyesyesyesyesyesyesyesyesyesyesyesyesyesyes

I can finally describe why the other music feels wrong.

"I want it to soar," I say to Joe. "I want us to feel like when they are dancing, they are flying. I want the same wonder and joy they feel in surgery to be felt in this dance. I want to capture ten years of extraordinary friendship, of true caring, of tribal warriors, of Ride or Dies. I want to capture the glory of Cristina Yang and everything she means to herself and everything she means to Meredith and everything she means to us. In one song, in one dance, in one scene."

Joe sits quietly a long beat. Then he says:

"In one song. In one dance. In one scene."

I nod. Joe nods back.

We sit silently for a really long time.

We say it at almost the same time.

"Season One."

And the music battle is over. No one wins. Everyone wins. We need to find a song from Season One. And it has to be a song that captures the feelings of joy and newness of two interns just getting to know surgery and each other.

The result is perfect.

Tegan and Sara's anthemic song "Where Does the Good Go." A song we played early on in Season One way back when we all thought we'd do a few episodes, have a little fun and part ways. Now we are all intertwined. I've held Joe's babies. My daughter Harper learned to walk in these editing room halls. The song evokes longing and nostalgia and joy and love and it's not too slow or too fast. It soars.

Joe and I find the perfect spot to transition their dancing into slow motion. We want to jump out of real time and then we swing overhead just as Tegan and Sara hit the chorus. We fiddle with it. It is never exactly right, it is never perfect. And yet it is flawless. It is everything we want it to be.

And then because we cannot let this moment pass too quickly, because we do not want to part these friends before we must, Joe and I do something we rarely ever do in the editing room:

We open up a full minute of uninterrupted screen time to

watch Cristina and Meredith express themselves in the best way these two brilliant women can without scalpels in their hands—we watch them dance it out.

I find myself tearing up the first time I see it. These dark and twisty sisters have gone the same distance I have. They are also no longer dark or twisty.

This dance is joyful. This dance is triumphant.

This dance is a celebration of what you can become.

It is everything I wanted it to be.

They are flying.

yesyesyesyesyesyesyesyesyesyesyesyesyesyesyesyesyes

I feel a lot of warmth for Pam and Ken. The fictional versions. I don't resent them. I'm grateful for them. They were great friends while I needed them. And whether or not any of the friendship was actually true, it was true for me. As much as Cristina was true for me. As much as the stories I wrote in my notebooks in middle school were true for me. As much as the pantry was true for me. They provided me with something necessary at the time. I felt bolstered by their friendship. By their loyalty. By the *idea* that I had these amazing friends, these members of my tribe, these gladiators at my back. Riding and Dying for me. Like Cristina, they made me braver, faster, stronger.

I make stuff up for living.

For a time, Pam and Ken had been what I needed for living. Cristina too. But I don't need them anymore.

The upside of culling people from my life is that my focus has become very clear. My vision has become razor sharp. I now work to see people, not as I'd rewrite them, but as they have written themselves. I see them for who they are. And for who I am with them. Because it's not merely about surrounding myself with people who treat me well. It's also about surrounding myself with people whose self-worth, self-respect and values inspire me to elevate my own behavior. People who require that I stay truthful and kind and not totally crazy. Not eating every single thing in sight. Not hiding. Not saying no. I want Ride or Dies who make me want to be better person.

I no longer have to make them up. I am surrounded by them.

My friends are the real deal.

The tribe I have now, the real live flesh-and-blood Ride or Die tribe that has been here with me all along, is the real deal. My world has been sifted down to just the finest individuals. My sisters. My Scott, my Gordon, my Zola. My Christopher. A very small handful of others. They cheer me on. They hold my hand. They shove me forward when I want to hide. They were telling me to say *Yes* all along.

They do not make me braver, faster, stronger. They tell me I already *am* braver, faster, stronger. They do not chase my demons and chop off their heads for me. They tell me I am capable of slaying my own demons. They do not gladiate for me. They tell me I can gladiate for myself.

They are Team Badassery.

All I have to do every day is believe them.

And be on time for my applause.

That fills me up more than having a *nation* full of imaginary Cristinas at my back.

Yes to the real people. Yes to the true friends. Yes to not needing to lay a single piece of track.

Ride or Die.

Every single time.

Ride or Die.

yesyesyesyesyesyesyesyesyesyesyesyesyesyesyesyes

Finally, the dance is over. Meredith and Cristina smile at each other. Cristina turns to go and then at the door, she turns back. She delivers her very last words. Her final piece of advice to the women of America.

"Don't let what he wants eclipse what you need. He is very dreamy," she says. "But he is not the sun. You are."

Her final piece of advice is not just for the women of America, I am now realizing, but also for me.

14

Yes to Who I Am

It's sometime in the late 1970s. I'm six years old, heading down an aisle, holding up the train of my big sister's gown. It's Delorse's wedding day. It's a beautiful day, an outdoor garden wedding. The entire way down the aisle, over the music of the wedding march, I can hear my sister whispering, "I'm not going to make it, I'm not going to make it."

She's walking on grass, you see, her heels are sinking into the earth, her dress weighs more than I do and she's nervous. Getting her down the aisle has become a Herculean task.

"I'm not going to make it, I'm not going to make it."

Beside her, his hand on hers, his voice calm, his steps steady, my father helps her take each step forward. "One foot in front of the other," he says.

Every single time she whispers "I'm not going to make it," he whispers back "One foot in front of the other."

"I'm not going to make it."

"One foot in front of the other."

"I'm not going to make it."

"One foot in front of the other . . ."

I carried my sister's train when I was just a little kid about thirty-five years ago. Before that, at four years old, I was a flower girl at my aunt Carolyn's wedding. I've been maid of honor twice. I've been best man once. In the many seasons of *Grey's Anatomy* and *Private Practice*, I have worked with our production teams to plan more than fourteen weddings and counting—I still pick every gown and choose every engagement ring and discuss every reception theme.

Back in 2009, when Betsy Beers got married in Venice, Italy, overlooking the Grand Canal, I had no designated role. But because I chose to basically tackle her, cuff her and drag her to a studio dressing room filled with wedding gowns in an effort to keep her from "just throwing on something navy," as had been her plan, I considered my role the most important one of all. Betsy has the willowy figure of a runway model; as Vera Wang was my witness, I would get her to use it. There could be no higher calling. The only woman to be married in Peggy Guggenheim's museum under her favorite painting as the sun set on Venice's Grand Canal *would* be wearing couture or I would die trying. You are welcome, Italy.

As I forced her to try on dress after dress hand-selected by the stylish hands of Mimi Melgaard, Betsy kept giving me the eye, equal parts amused and horrified at the dreamlike joy on my face.

Betsy and I have worked together for almost fifteen years. We think the secret to our ability to spend so many hours together without a single homicide is the fact that we are exact opposites. She's tall and thin and white and Waspy. I am short and curvy and black and Catholic. The angrier I get, the calmer I become. The angrier she gets, the louder she becomes. She has an encyclopedic memory for TV, films, literature, pop culture, music, you name it. I often do not remember where my watch is until someone points out that it is on my wrist. We are opposites. Still, she seems flummoxed by my giddiness over fluffy white dresses. She finds the concept of a white dress atrocious. That I could be giddy about a fluffy white dress—that I could have *such* a different feeling about weddings than she does—flummoxes her.

After I come very close to spontaneously combusting from excitement one time too many, she can't take it.

"How can you be this pee-your-pants excited?" she asks, yanking off a frilly confection that would look ridiculous on any human.

"Because I love weddings!" I shriek. The proximity to all these wedding gowns is giving me some kind of weird contact high. It's the same feeling I get when I am about to crush someone at Scrabble. Or badminton. Or knitting.

I mean, I *love* weddings.

I love weddings.

Of course I do. They're parties. And I love parties.

But I *really* love weddings.

LOVE them. ADORE them.

The flowers, the candles, the vows, the themes, the dresses.

I can't get enough of them.

I can tell you exactly what my wedding would be like, what my dress would look like, the food I'd serve . . . oh, I have planned enough weddings to know just what kind of wedding I'd want.

There is just one problem. And that day, as Betsy steps out of the dressing room, flawlessly working the perfect wedding gown, she says it.

"I do not see how you can love weddings this much and not want to get married."

Oh yeah. That.

In 2009, I don't want to get married.

That's kind of the problem. Well . . . actually, no. That's not the problem.

The problem is that it is now 2014. The problem is that I am supposed to be getting married in the summer. About eight months from the time I start the Year of Yes.

And I still do not want to get married.

I do not think I'm ever going to want to get married.

THAT is the problem.

yesyesyesyesyesyesyesyesyesyesyesyesyesyesyesyes

I have always known that I wanted to be a mother. I have always known that I wanted to adopt. I have known these things with one hundred percent certainty. Like you know about the sunrise. Like you know about the seasons. These were facts. The way I have known I will age beautifully. The way I know I'm a writer. Motherhood felt so true inside me that it never occurred to me to question it.

I assume some people feel that way about marriage. I think they do.

I don't.

Never have.

While I didn't do a lot of playing as a kid, Sandie did play. As the only small kids growing up in a house full of teenagers, my sister Sandie found herself forced to turn to me as a playmate. Older than me by two years, she'd wrangle me out of the pantry or take the book from my hands. And she'd make me play with her. But she didn't play in the way other kids seemed to want to play. Sandie did not want to play kickball or ride her bike really fast or dig in the dirt or squeal in a group of girls chasing boys around. No. Sandie was interested in elaborate games of pretend.

Well . . .

Elaborate games of pretending she was my mother.

She used construction paper and crayons to craft her own

little kitchen, and then we played *Making Dinner and Washing the Dishes.* When my mother saw how intent Sandie was, Sandie received a tiny apron, a tiny china tea set and a real tiny Bundt pan that my mom allowed her to use to bake real tiny cakes in the actual stove. Once a week, Sandie would carefully lay out our large collection of doll clothes on the kitchen table, handmade price tags taped to each one. Then we'd stand outside the screen door staring at the clock until one of my older sisters obligingly yelled, "The store is open!" That was our signal to hurry inside and be the first get to the sale merchandise. At some point, a pretend salesclerk would pretend-say something snobby to Sandie, something with slightly racist undertones. And Sandie would tell off the pretend salesclerk so fiercely and smartly and with such dignity that the clerk, reduced to tears, would end up chasing Sandie through the store offering to sell her the dress for cheaper. That always led to Sandie's demanding to speak to the pretend manager. This game was called *Mom Shopping at the Department Store.*

Sandie was given a tiny pink and white Singer sewing machine one Christmas that I think was supposed to be a toy but in Sandie's hands became like her own mini *Project Runway* kit. She sewed clothes for our dolls—truly impressive, fashionable, well-made clothes. She explained to me the importance of a quality product and why the cheap stuff at the mall was not worth it. This was called *Mom Sewing.*

For a long time I played with her obediently, following her lead. But as I got older, all bets were off . . .

My Cara doll—because in the seventies if you had a black Barbie, her name was Cara and she had short hair, and then in the eighties her name was Christie and she had long hair with gold highlights—anyway, my Cara doll spent most of her time hanging out at college with her friend Cara II, who coincidentally looked exactly like Cara, discussing her plans for skiing in Gstaad (Gstaad always sounded cool to me) and trying to decide between becoming a governess and traveling with her rich aunt as a companion (*Little Women* was big for me then). At some point, Ken would inevitably show up to ask her out. Cara never giggled and put on the tiny bridal gown that my sister had painstakingly sewn for her. And she never went out with Ken.

When I first got Ken, I had examined him carefully. I was weirded out by his strange smooth square pelvis and his painted-on hair. And his head . . . that was Ken's downfall.

Cara never dated that Ken. Instead, she popped Ken's head off and stored her many pairs of shoes inside his hollow skull for safekeeping. Then she'd pop his head back on and make him drive her to the spy organization she was secretly running with her archenemy, Nancy Drew. Ken's hollow head was functional *and* ornamental.

I did not want to make tiny Bundt cakes or sew dresses. Or wear aprons or shop. I was not interested in playing reality. I wanted to spend my time, well . . . making stuff up. Telling stories. Living in my imagination. And nowhere in there was marriage part of it.

Oh, but the brides . . .

Brides became my everything the first time I saw Maria in *The Sound of Music*. She left the convent, she had a billion children, that captain dude was hot and her wedding dress was *fierce*.

I love romance. I love love.

I love dating the non-Kens of the world, the men with something more inside their heads than air. I love being in a relationship. I love interesting men.

I love my client having meetings. Mmmkay?

But.

Married?

Who cared?

"But, Shonda, what if he's The One? What if you are MFEO? What if he's your soul mate?"

Sigh.

yesyesyesyesyesyesyesyesyesyesyesyesyesyesyesyesyes

This is how well matched my parents are.

In 1994, I am graduating with an MFA from the University of Southern California film school, and so my parents fly down for the ceremony.

I insist that they stay with me in my little apartment in not one of the nicest sections of Los Angeles. They gamely agree. That night, I give them my bed and I lie down on the floor to sleep.

It's quiet, it's dark, we've all been lying there for maybe thirty or forty minutes. I'm thinking they are asleep. I'm almost asleep. Then from the darkness my mother's voice floats up.

"You know, I was thinking," she says.

Not a question. A statement.

And my dad responds immediately. I was wrong about them being asleep.

"About what?"

And my mom says—

Wait. Let's be clear that I'm going to get this completely wrong because I don't know ANYTHING about this topic, okay? Anyway . . .

—my mom says something like, "I was thinking about Maslov's theory of psychosexual representation and how it relates to Stockholm syndrome."

I am lying on the floor thinking, "WHAT?"

Because I was thinking about maybe . . . candy.

Did I mention my mom is a brainiac PhD?

I wait for my dad to answer. I wait, wondering how is he going to kindly tell my mom no one knows what she is talking about and to please go to sleep.

YEAR *of* YES   269

But that is not what happens.

Listen to this. *Just listen.*

"I was thinking about Maslov's theory of psychosexual representation and how it relates to Stockholm syndrome," my mom says.

And my dad responds:

"I was thinking about that too!!"

Like that. With two exclamation points in his voice. And then my parents proceed to have a long, enthusiastic conversation about whatever the hell this topic is about.

That's how well matched they are.

Because my dad was thinking about that too.

My mom was thinking about it. And my dad was thinking about it too. And they both found it interesting.

They are always thinking about the same things and finishing each other's sentences. They consistently follow each other around their house from room to room. Like ducks who have imprinted on each other.

They met on a blind date. It must have been an incredible blind date. It seems to have never ended.

They are partners, travel companions, best friends, an intellectual society of two, fellow sports fans, perfectly complementary, and after fifty-whatever years, they are still sweethearts, madly in love. People think I'm exaggerating about my parents' marriage until they meet them. Once you meet them, you'll see it too. My parents are the perfect example of what marriage should be. They understand the work of marriage and seem to believe in its constancy. To them, it is a journey that has twists, turns, bumps and possibly detours, but no end. There are no exit ramps. And they don't care. They are too busy having fun.

I grew up with a front-row seat to what a happy, healthy marriage looks like. Never perfect, constantly evolving, always united.

My parents are the marriage jackpot.

My parents make marriage look like the most delightful fifty-plus-year-long date. My parents make you think raising six kids and growing old together will be some kind of dance party. I worship their marriage. I revere and respect it. I am smug about it to all of my friends.

They are MFEO: Made For Each Other.

They are soul mates.

I still do not want to get married.

I tell myself that this is because they have the perfect marriage. That their example is too perfect. That if I just meet someone who makes me think I can have a marriage that great . . .

I told myself I had an open mind. Until I hit forty, the fact that I didn't want to get married was just this thing that floated through my mind from time to time. It wasn't even real. It was just a theory. I never even said it out loud. Not to anyone. Why would I? Judging by some of the reactions I've gotten to stories I've written for my characters on TV, a woman not wanting to marry or not wanting to have children is cause for a good old-fashioned witch trial.

People really do not like it when you decide to step off the road and climb the mountain instead. It seems to make even the people who mean well nervous.

"We just want you to be happy," confused friends would say to me anxiously whenever I seemed completely content to be single.

I kept my feelings to myself. I didn't mention it to friends or family. I didn't mention it to men I was dating. I thought, "Who knows, what do I know? I'll change my mind. Maybe I am wrong. Maybe marriage is something I want and I don't know I want it. Be open."

So I was open. As open as I could be while building a life, career and family that didn't require a husband.

And then . . .

yesyesyesyesyesyesyesyesyesyesyesyesyesyesyesyes

I am going to talk about this *without* talking about this. As much as I can. Be kind about that. I let you all up in my business. But this? Not just my business. And here? I do change more than a few details. I change all kinds of details. I toss in some glitter and take out some of the sparkles. I want to get the point across—I do not want to get across any actual facts that involve another person.

Are we clear?

Anyway, it was my fault, really.

The whole marriage thing. I started it. I never meant to. I didn't plan it. I just . . .

He's a great guy. He's funny and smart and really cute.

I was enthusiastic about him. I'd known him for years. He loved my kids. My family adored him. My friends liked him. We had fun, we laughed, we talked. He loved me. I loved him. The whole thing was great.

I was enthusiastic.

I was really enthusiastic.

Do you feel what's about to happen?

I didn't. I do *now*. I can see it clearly now. But then . . . I didn't see it coming.

There's a point in every relationship where the question is, where is this going? How serious is this? What's next?

I never ask those questions. Which I hear is rare for a woman. But I don't. Because I don't care about the answers. I'm all about, where are we now? What's happening now?

But someone in the relationship always ends up asking these questions. Where is this going? How serious is this? What's next?

He wants to know.

I'm enthusiastic.

But I don't want to talk about what's next.

But he wants to know.

And I'm pretty sure the reason he wants to know is because I'm enthusiastic. My enthusiasm has allowed him to wonder.

Talk about a difficult conversation. And before the Year of Yes, I don't know what to do about difficult conversations.

I'm nervous, I'm stressed. But I don't want to be ambivalent. I want to have some answers. I care about the answers because HE cares about the answers.

Maybe I do want to get married. Maybe marriage is awesome.

Yes. Clearly. Marriage is awesome.

I tell Linda Lowy all about how awesome marriage is. She's been married forever. But still, I lecture her. I give her a high-pitched *Scandal*-paced monologue on how fabulous marriage is for people. She stares at me. Later, she will tell me I had the craziest, swirliest eyes she has ever seen on a human person. But I feel satisfied. I think I have it all together.

Before I started the Year of Yes, I thought a lot of crazy, swirly things about myself. But clearly, I need a little help. Clearly, I've got a problem.

And so, without asking, without telling—it's all don't ask, don't tell up in there—the storyteller is called off the bench in my brain and steps up to the plate. And—hell yes, I'm going all sports metaphor on you—hits a home run on the first pitch.

The storyteller solves the problem. My inner liar cleans it all up. We sit down around the campfire, my storyteller and

I, and we spin tales about weddings on ranches in Montana and we talk about how marriage is good once you're in it and how perfectly matched we are and how of course this is going to be great and how we are imprinted on each other like two ducks.

I lay some track.

Oh, the track I lay.

For a train that is . . .

. . . *that's* the thing.

There *is* no train.

There's no crew waiting to build a set. There's no budget that has to be kept. No actors to film.

I am laying track in a ghost town for a ghost train.

I am laying track on a route to nowhere for a train that ain't coming.

Only I don't know it yet. I still think I hear that train whistle in the distance. It'll be here any minute now . . .

And so I stay enthusiastic.

Marriage!! How great is that?!

(breathe, breathe)

. . . two ducks imprinted on each other . . .

One foot in front of the other. I'm not going to make it.

Us together *for the rest of our lives*.

One foot in front of the other. I'm not going to make it.

. . . two ducks imprinted on each other . . .

He is so happy. I am so happy. Just . . .

One foot in front of the other. I'm not going to make it.

I think of Delorse, thirty-five years into her marriage with Jeff. I think of my parents, a lifetime into theirs. I imagine me two months into my marriage and I get a headache.

Let's wait, I say. To tell our families and friends. Until after life with my newest baby settles down. Until after our families have met. Until after Christmas.

Until after, until after, until after . . .

One foot in front of the other. One foot in front of the other. One foot in front of the other.

I'm not going to make it.

Right now, remember, we are pre–Year of Yes. So I do what I always did when I am stressed. I started eating.

I eat. And eat. And eat. I put food on top of food on top of food. Like I said, I am the fattest I have ever been. He doesn't mind. He loves me. His love transcends the superficial. He's an incredible human being.

The more incredible he is, the more food I shove in my face hole.

People keep telling me that I am glowing.

Because I am in love, they say!

Because I am fat and sweaty, I say!

Everyone is so incredibly happy that I am with him. They love him. They can't get enough of loving him.

Side note: the praise I received for having a guy everyone hoped I would marry eclipsed *any and all* praise or congrat-

ulations or excitement that accompanied the births of my
children and any of my many career accomplishments. It was
stunning. The presence of a man at my side had people as ap-
oplectic with joy as those old videos of people seeing Michael
Jackson perform live. Where they are screaming and crying.

Okay, not screaming and crying.

But seriously.

They were almost screaming and crying.

A dude. Versus three children; an entire night of television;
a Peabody Award; a Golden Globe; lifetime achievement
awards from the DGA, the WGA and GLAAD; fourteen
NAACP Image Awards; three AFI Awards; a Harvard medal;
and being inducted into the Broadcasting Hall of Fame—to
name just a few of my many accomplishments.

A *dude*.

He's a great guy. One of the best. Clooney *wishes*.

But since I am not Dr. Frankenstein and thus had no hand
in his creation, I would prefer not to be celebrated for his
presence.

It's oogey.

Like my street value went up because a guy wanted me.

You know what's a bigger taboo than being fat?

Not wanting to get married.

Remind me to start a revolution about that later.

*yes*yes*yes*yes*yes*yes*yes*yes*yes*yes*yes*yes*yes*yes*yes*yes

As the Year of Yes gets under way, I begin to unwind my mind from the story that we are two ducks, that we are imprinted. Because we are not. I knew we are not. Because I was lying awake at night. Panicking.

He would move in here? With me? And the kids? Live here? With me?

I would have to talk to him all the time. See him every single day. Be aware of him. Hand him even more of my energy and focus. It is incredibly hard to fit him in now. And I don't mean that as an insult. I mean that as truth. All of my free time, I spend with the kids and then my friends and my family. There's a certain amount of time alone I need just to have the brain space to write, to have what I call mental pantry time. I already give up some time from each to see him.

He kindly offers, "I can just hang out here while you write. We don't have to talk. I just want to be with you."

You and I are close friends now, reader. So you know how I feel about writing.

Writing is the hum. Writing is laying track. Writing is the high.

Now imagine that hum, that high, that track to be laid is behind a door. And that door is five miles away. Those five miles are just . . . writing crap and doodling and trying to have an idea and surfing the internet and hoping like hell not to get so distracted that you give up. Worse? Those five miles are lined with brownies and cupcakes and episodes of *Game of Thrones* and Idris Elba waiting to talk to only you and really good novels to read.

Every time I sit down to write, I have to mentally run those five miles past all of that to get to that door. It's a long, hard five-mile run. Sometimes I am almost dead by the time I reach the door.

That's why I have to keep doing it.

The more often I run the five miles, the fitter I become. And the fitter I become, the easier the run begins to feel and the less fresh and exciting all that stuff on the side of the road seems. I mean, how long has it been there? More important, as I get fitter, I can run faster. And the faster I can run, the faster I can get to that door.

The faster you can too, writers out there.

When you sit down to write every day, it becomes easier and easier to tap into that creative space inside your mind.

The faster I can get to that door, the quicker I can get to the good stuff.

Behind that door is the good stuff.

So when I reach the door and open it . . . that's when my creativity clicks in and that special spot in my brain starts working and I go from exertion to exultation and suddenly I can write forever and ever and ever and eve—

And then someone opens the door and asks me if I want coffee or water and I am FIVE MILES AWAY all over again.

I grit my teeth and try to smile and say *No thank you, see, I have coffee AND water both already, right here.* And then I start running that five miles all over.

That happens roughly thirty-five times a day at the office.

Someone turns off my hum. It's always for a good reason. But I still have to sit on my hands to avoid the murder charges currently happening in an alternate universe.

Imagine that happening at home, gentle reader. With someone who loves you and isn't trying to bother you.

I don't have to imagine it. I know it all too well.

I have children. Any working mother knows. But it's one thing if they shut off my hum. I would willingly grit my teeth and smile for them all day. I would stand in front of a bus for them. I would fight a lion for them. They are my kids.

I try to imagine if it weren't my kids. I try to imagine willingly adding him to the mix.

Why would I do that to myself? To him?

It makes me feel trapped. Caged. I know, I know. This makes me seem like a monster. *Someone loves you so much that they want to be with you, Shonda! What is your problem? I just don't get you!*

You know who gets me? Who feels me on this topic?

Cristina Yang.

I gave her my ambivalence about marriage. I gave her my passion for work. I gave her my love for something greater than any romance, something that draws her focus more than any guy—a creative genius floating forever out of reach that she will never stop trying to capture.

Her true love? Her soul mate? Her MFEO?

Surgery.

Why marry the guy when you can have the Chocolate Factory?

He loves me. I love him. Still. I can't imagine giving him any more attention. I try. I just can't imagine it.

I finally speak up. And I say that I want to push back not just a wedding but any *talk* of a wedding.

For how long?

For one whole year.

That does not go over well. But he accepts it. Because he truly is a fantastic, kind and understanding person. I'm the one still on edge. Because I know this isn't it. I know I'm postponing the real conversation.

In this Year of Yes, this Yes is the hardest Yes.

Say yes, I tell myself. *Say yes to telling your truth.*

I talk to my Ride or Dies. They are solemn. Concerned. But supportive. My tribe is behind me.

So I do it. I say it. To him. To his face. For the first time.

"I do not want to get married. I may never want to get married. I am pretty positive that I absolutely will never want to get married. Well. Maybe when Beckett is out of college. Or when I'm seventy-five."

He's stunned. And rightly so.

He wants to know why.

I talk for a long time. About the traditional reasons for marriage no longer existing for an independent woman. About how marriage is a piece of paper, a binding contract used to protect property and assets, and a lot of times it is rightly used to protect women's rights if they have been raising children and find themselves left without an income. Marriage is a financial partnership. Marriage has nothing to do with love. Love is a choice we can make every day. Romantic love as a path to marriage is a fairly new concept, I tell him. And it is a foolish one.

I tell him I don't believe in divorce. Ever.

I tell him that I have seen a great, fantastic joining of both marriage and romantic love up close and personal with my parents and because of that, I know what marriage plus sustained love looks like and how much work it takes.

I take a deep breath and tell him my first love is writing. Writing and I are MFEO. I tell him that my well of energy is only so deep and that I happily pour that energy into writing and raising my daughters, and so I would never be pouring the energy into a devoted marriage in the way I know from our conversations he imagines a marriage would be. I tell him that he would resent me and grow to hate me if we got married and I did not make him a priority above my work. And I have no ability to downgrade my creativity in my soul. I have no desire to do so either.

I say, let's be more bohemian about this. Let's just let love be love and let go of all the definitions and the expectations. Let's stop thinking about marriage as the finish line, let's re-define what a life together is for ourselves. Let's be free, let's not be bound by rules.

I want to say all of this.

I don't say all of this.

I say some of it. I don't get all of it out. Because he looks so disappointed. And confused.

He says, "But . . . but . . . I thought you were much more traditional than this."

And that is when I realize: *I am the train.*

I am the train.

I laid the tracks.

For the train that is *me.*

I am the story rumbling down those tracks and out of sight. I am the falsehood. I made me up. I laid those tracks and built those sets and filmed myself and I whistled right into the station. And boy, was that train a good ride. I give good story. I created me into whatever it was he was look-ing for.

And that creation has little in common with the person I see every day in the mirror.

I'm old. And I like to lie.

Who knew I was lying to both of us?

The role of Shonda is being played by . . . Shonda.

yesyesyesyesyesyesyesyesyesyesyesyesyesyesyesyesyes

I'd like to be able to tell you that I staggered out of that relationship, devastated and broken.

I didn't.

I know I told you not to come up into my book and judge me. But here, right here on this page? You are free to judge. I won't cop an attitude and toss you out of my book. You can judge.

See. The thing about this big momentous breakthrough I had that crystallized who I am and forever changed my life? This breakthrough only happened to me. I had a breakthrough. Someone else got broken. So while I was busy having epiphanies, a horrible thing was happening to a perfectly wonderful human being. I may have been growing and changing but I was also taking someone's dream and plan for the future and setting it on fire. That the price of my joy was another person's pain is something I'll forgive myself for. One day.

But then, on that day? Right when it ended, I couldn't feel any of that. All I could feel was . . . overwhelming relief. Joy.

So like I said, you are free to judge. You go on ahead and you do some judging. You'll want to. Because I gotta tell you, I didn't just walk out of that relationship . . .

I danced.

I *danced it out*. Happier than I'd been in a long time.

yesyesyesyesyesyesyesyesyesyesyesyesyesyesyesyes

When I see Delorse, I'm beaming. Glowing. Lighter. Happy.

"Why are you so cheerful?" she asks.

"We broke up because I don't ever want to get married!"

Her brow furrows. I am quite literally shaking my groove thing around the family room. My mother calls this "airing out your behind," and when she says that, we are supposed to stop. But my mother is not here, so I bust out my best eighties dance moves: the Running Man, the Cabbage Patch . . .

Delorse stares at me. My daughter Emerson is on her lap. She stares at me too. Delorse waves a hand in my direction, capturing all of my moves in one gesture.

"This. Is this some Year of Yes thing happening?"

"Yeah!" And I tell her what happened as I dance.

"So," she says slowly when I'm done, "you are this happy because you said yes to not getting married."

I stop airing out my behind. I sit down. I'm quiet for a long moment.

"No. I think that I am this happy because I realized that I *really* don't want the fairy tale. I mean, I had it. I mean, I was there. I already have a great career, great kids, wonderful home, terrific life. And now, here was the great guy. I had it, I was going to *have it all*. I'm supposed to want it all. It's supposed to complete me. Getting the great guy is the series finale. Part of me secretly thought that maybe I was just being obstinate—that if I just did what I was supposed to do, if I got married, I would end up being happier. And everyone was thrilled for me. It would have been so simple. The wedding was right there. The amazing guy was right there. The happy was right there. *And I didn't want it.*"

And I moonwalk out of the room. Delorse stares after me. I know she doesn't understand. I'll explain it to her later. Right now, I have to dance.

This yes is a big one for me.

You ready?

My happy ending is not the same as your happy ending. And yours is not the same as my sister Delorse's or my sister Sandie's or Zola's or Betsy's or Gordon's or Scott's or Jenny McCarthy's. Everyone has their own version.

We all spend our lives kicking the crap out of ourselves for not being this way or that way, not having this thing or that thing, not being like this person or that person.

For not living up to some standard we think applies across the board to all of us.

We all spend our lives trying to follow the same path, live by the same rules.

I think we believe that happiness lies in following the same list of rules.

In being more like everyone else.

That? Is wrong.

There is no list of rules.

There is one rule.

The rule is: there are no rules.

Happiness comes from living as *you* need to, as you *want* to. As your inner voice tells you to. Happiness comes from being who you actually are instead of who you think you are supposed to be.

Being traditional is not traditional anymore.

It's funny that we still think of it that way.

Normalize your lives, people.

You don't want a baby? Don't have one.

I don't want to get married? I won't.

You want to live alone? Enjoy it.

You want to love someone? Love someone.

Don't apologize. Don't explain. Don't ever feel less than.

When you feel the need to apologize or explain who you are, it means the voice in your head is telling you the wrong story. Wipe the slate clean. And rewrite it.

No fairy tales.

Be your own narrator.

And go for a happy ending.

One foot in front of the other.

You will make it.

15

Yes to Beautiful

I am standing on an apple box.

The sturdy wooden crate traditionally used to hold fruit is serving as my platform, making me tall enough so that the light hits my face at the right angle. The light hitting my face at the right angle, I've been told, is very important.

This isn't my area of expertise. So when the camera assistant points to the apple box, I obediently step up on it. I stand on the apple box and I don't move. I wait. Someone will tell me what to do next, right?

Behind me hangs a large piece of dark fabric, a simple and elegant backdrop. In front of me there are thick snakes of electrical cable, high lights with color filters, a deep sea of crew members forming an intense obstacle course. A couple of sturdy guys with Southern accents work to place the camera in a specific location, moving it an inch or two in search of precision according to some unseen plan.

Deep in the back of the room, I can see well-dressed men and women hovering around the corners of the room, staying out of the way of equipment as they talk to one another in low voices. These are the suits—the army of studio publicists and personal publicists and managers and magazine executives required to make sure the day runs smoothly and on schedule. I catch a glimpse of Chris—Chris #1, my publicist—back there.

I scan the room to my left, taking in the makeshift wall that has been raised to separate the dressing room from the rest of the studio. From behind it, I can hear the sound of Ellen Pompeo's laughter on one side of the room and the low calm tones of Viola Davis's voice on the other. Somewhere in the middle, I know, is Kerry Washington.

I am here with the leading ladies of Thursday night. Ellen, Kerry, Viola and I are doing a photo shoot for *Entertainment Weekly*. I'm about to become a cover girl for one of the most popular magazines in the country.

Stand on this apple box?

Hell yeah, I will.

If you want me to stand on my head, I will give it a try.

Finally, I spot him. The man I'm searching for. The photographer. James White. He's huddled off to one side with his team. They are staring at me, conferring in low voices. Heads tilted to one side, examining me, dissecting what they see.

I stand as tall as I can, hoping to make their view more pleasing. I suck in my stomach as much as it will suck; I try to put on a face that looks like some version of confident and fierce. I try to look like a supermodel. Oh, that is *not* gonna happen. I have to shake my head, amused that I even wanted to try.

But for a split second, I feel like I want to run. I actually consider it. Maybe I will. Maybe I will just turn around and run.

Yes. I can write a chapter about it.

Yes to *running*.

The thought makes me snort. The snort makes Cathy frown at me.

"Stop it."

Cathy is a genius makeup artist and right now she's trying to make sure my eyes look perfect. So when she says "Stop it," she's being bossy for a good reason. She's really saying, "If you laugh, you shake, and if you shake, this long pointy thing I am holding up to your eye will stab you in the eyeball and you will never laugh again."

I know this because we've been working together for a long time now—years. We have a shorthand.

I sigh at her. Nostalgic. Awed.

"Can you *believe*?"

I mean *this*. Where we are. What we are doing. The magazine cover. I mean the idea that a year ago, this would have seemed preposterous. Now, it seems fun.

She grins at me. Cathy and my hairstylist Verlyn have had a front-row seat to this journey. During my shakiest early days of the challenge, they cheered me on and reminded me that the Year of Yes was a good idea. They have seen me stripped bare, they have seen me raw. They know every wrinkle, gray hair and flaw. Before every interview, public appearance or photo shoot, my eyes find them and wait for the slight nod of approval that means I look okay, that I am safe to proceed. Along with my stylist Dana, they are my Ride or Die glam team.

Cathy beams at me, glowing. Warm.

"After the week you've had?" she says. "Yes, Shonda. I *can* believe."

yesyesyesyesyesyesyesyesyesyesyesyesyesyesyesyes

It has been an uncommon week in an uncommon year. A week of new portraits finding their rightful places on the walls of my brain.

Last Monday, I stood in a recording booth and got to become a statue.

Literally.

The city of Chicago had asked various writers to write pieces that would illuminate artworks around the city. These written pieces were to be recorded as spoken word files, digitally accessible to anyone with a smartphone. The artwork I was assigned was Miró's *The Sun, The Moon and One Star*. An ungainly thirty-nine-foot bell-like structure with a fork for a head, the piece stands in Brunswick Plaza. When first installed, it was declared hideous and was mocked, but it has since grown to be beloved and is now known by the affectionate nickname "Miss Chicago."

I wrote a monologue that gave Miss Chicago a shy, unattractive feminine personality that slowly gains strength and spirit. I was in that booth to record the monologue for the public. I was there to become the voice of Miss Chicago. That moment is frozen in time for me forever, a small but mighty portrait on my wall. As I stood there, alone before the microphone, speaking the words I had written for the statue, I had to pause to steady myself. I was unexpectedly moved at saying out loud, at *owning*, some of the lines I'd so easily handed to a statue.

"I am different. I am an original. And like everyone else, I am here to take up space in the universe. I do so with pride."

*yes*yes*yes*yes*yes*yes*yes*yes*yes*yes*yes*yes*yes*yes*yes*yes*yes

On Tuesday, a new painting went up inside this head of mine. I'd found myself once again at the Beverly Hilton Hotel at the TCAs. ABC was closing their presentation to

the critics with a TGIT panel. Viola, Kerry, Ellen, the other
producers and I took goofy selfies just before stepping onstage. I wore a bright kelly green Oscar de la Renta dress and
sat dead center. I can't tell you how long the panel lasted; I
am never sure of the timing on those things. But I can tell
you I was chatty. I can tell you it felt more like my living
room than a firing squad. Someone asked me who would
play me in the movie of my life, a question that still makes
me laugh out loud at the horror. At the cocktail party that
took place that same evening, journalist after journalist came
up to me to ask questions about the shows and then leaned
in to say things like:

"You know, this is the first time I have ever seen you smile
up there."

"If I only knew your secret . . ."

"You are just so . . . different this year."

First. Only. Different.

Yes.

Yes, I am.

yes yes yes yes yes yes yes yes yes yes yes yes yes yes yes yes

Last Friday, I made my way up the California coast to The
Promised Land. Which is the name of Oprah's home. As if
you didn't know that. That's like not knowing the White
House is called the White House.

I had been invited to The Promised Land to film an epi-sode of the Oprah Winfrey Network's *Super Soul Sunday*.

I sat with Oprah for the interview. And I survived it.

I did better than survive it.

If you call me up and you ask, "Hey Shonda, what was it like being interviewed by Oprah?"

Good question.

I'm glad you asked.

Get comfortable and I'll tell you all about it.

BECAUSE I CAN TOTALLY REMEMBER EVERY DETAIL.

I remember the experience. I was mentally present. My soul did not leave my body in preparation for my inevitable death.

I was relaxed. I was comfortable. There were no nerves. The interview was just plain fun.

You heard me.

I had a flat-out, truly, really good time doing that inter-view.

A nice big painting hung itself on the walls of my brain and it has stayed there.

And it wasn't just because Oprah was awesome. Oprah is without a doubt, the best talk show host on the planet and incredibly smart, insightful and kind. And she *was* awesome. But we have established that she has always been awesome and still, before the Year of Yes, the old Shonda would have suffered some kind of nuclear panic attack, resulting in total amnesia.

Oprah will always be amazing in this scenario.

The difference was me.

I had no armor on. I had nothing to hide. I was worried about nothing.

I was . . . fearless.

And so we had a conversation. We had a chat. We talked.

What had I always been so afraid of?

What had I been guarding?

What was I so nervous about?

yesyesyesyesyesyesyesyesyesyesyesyesyesyesyesyes

And now I'm here being photographed for the cover of *EW*.

Another painting for the walls.

"I think it's time," Cathy tells me as she removes the tissues stuffed in the neck of my evening gown and backs away.

And suddenly James is standing in front of me. He's got a camera slung over his shoulder and I can see two or three more cameras on a cart waiting to be used.

James has a friendly, open face. I like him immediately. He reaches out, takes my hands in his and looks at me. I let my body relax, let my eyes focus on his. I have learned enough about being photographed to know that I need to be here in this room with James at this moment. Nowhere else.

"Are you ready?" he asks.

I take a deep breath.

Am I ready?

Am I?

I take another deep breath and look at James.

"Yes," I say. "Yes, I am ready."

James grins. Squeezes my hand and winks, reassuring.

"Let's do this," he says, and heads away to get another camera.

yesyesyesyesyesyesyesyesyesyesyesyesyesyesyesyesyes

Days earlier, I tried to explain to Delorse the magnitude of what she had done for me that Thanksgiving morning a year and a half ago. I tried to thank her, I tried to tell her that she changed my life. That she *saved* my life. While I talked, Delorse stared at me, her head tilted to one side. Waiting politely, but her face indicating how ridiculous she thought I sounded.

"Shonda," she said when I finally stopped talking, "I didn't do anything. You did all the work. It was like . . ."

Here Delorse paused. She often takes long pauses that act as epic cliffhangers when you are discussing important topics. She went to my refrigerator and dug around until she found a peach. She washed it. Dried it. I'm not kidding.

"It was like you needed permission," she said finally. Then she shrugged. "I'm your big sister. I gave you permission. Not a big deal."

I nodded. I was heading away when she spoke again.

"I'm extremely proud of you," she said quietly. "You were joyless. All you ever did was sleep. Literally. And metaphorically. You were asleep. I was worried. Life is short. Yours seemed really, really short. And now you have completely transformed. You're alive. You're living. Some people never do that."

And then she put her purse on her shoulder and walked out my kitchen door.

This sister of mine.

yesyesyesyesyesyesyesyesyesyesyesyesyesyesyesyes

The one thing I have learned is that I don't know ANYTHING. If someone had told me on that Thanksgiving morning in 2013 that I would be an entirely different person today, I would have laughed in their face. And yet . . . here I am.

One hundred twenty-seven pounds thinner.

Several toxic people lighter.

Closer to my family.

A better mother.

A better friend.

A happier boss.

A stronger leader.

A more creative writer.

A more honest person—both with myself and with everyone else in my life. More adventurous. More open. Braver. And kinder. To others. But also to myself. The cruelty with which I treated myself is no longer tolerated.

The pantry door is open. I am out among the living.

Climbing another mountain.

Looking for another view.

Hanging painting after painting on the walls in there.

yesyesyesyesyesyesyesyesyesyesyesyesyesyesyesyes

There's a fan blowing on my face. Beyoncé is blaring out of the speakers in the ceiling. James is photographing me. All his guys are around, all eyes on my every move. They are peering at me, adjusting lights. Adjusting focus. I am too busy dancing it out to be self-conscious.

James gestures and suddenly one of his big guys is by my side. He puts down a bigger apple box. Holds out his hand and guides me as I step onto it. I look to James. He gestures for the volume of the music to be lowered for a moment. Then he directs me into position.

"Step forward. Turn your face, just a bit. Now, I don't want you to feel stiff or like you can't enjoy yourself—I love it— but do you feel that warmth on your face? I need you to always feel that."

I nod.

James points to someone and Beyoncé is back and he is shooting shot after shot after shot and I am dancing. I am Crazy in Love and then I am Drunk in Love and then I Run the World. And as I do, as I dance, I look down on everyone from my spot on top of my little mound of apple boxes. Cathy is out there dancing with me and everyone is smiling and the room is just a wave of energy. I raise my hands, running them through my hair, and turn my face into the warmth of the light.

"I am on my own mountain standing in my own sun," I think to myself.

James moves in, photographing my face close up just as I burst out laughing at the thought.

And James and the guys around him laugh right back. The camera never stops shooting images. Queen Bey never stops singing.

James grins, glances at the monitor.

"You are beautiful!" he shouts at me.

You are beautiful.

James says it like it's a foregone conclusion. He shouts it. And so I decide not to disagree with him. I decide to believe him. James is clearly a brilliant man. James *knows* of what he speaks.

"Yes," I whisper to myself, "I am beautiful."

James looks at me.

"Do you have more in you?"

I grin.

"YES."

Immediately James raises his camera, moving in again, taking photo after photo.

"Keep dancing," he orders. "You will not believe what I am seeing!"

And so I dance it out. I dance it out on my mountain in my sun as if my life depends on it. Because it does.

And James is wrong about believing. Because when I see the photos later, I absolutely do believe what I am seeing. The woman I see may be new, but I know her well. I like her. I like who she is. I like who she's becoming.

I love her.

Staring at those photos, I know now that is what my Year of Yes has always been about. Love.

It's just love, is all.

That little girl with the canned vegetables opens that pantry door just enough to peer through the sliver of door into sunlight. She too sees this beautiful woman bathed in light wearing the red dress with the big smile on her face.

She approves. She loves her too.

Who I was. Who I am.

It's just love.

I can't wait to find out who I will be when next Thanksgiving rolls around.

Whoever I'll be, I will be beautiful.

Because I may be an old liar, but I will be a beautiful old liar.

I will be happy.

I will be worth it.

Worth the Chocolate Factory.

Always a work in progress.

Always dancing.

Always in the sun.

Yes.

Always dancing in the sun.

Yes.

Yes.

Yes.

Acknowledgments

So many hands, so much help. In so many ways, so many people were of invaluable assistance to me both with this book and with the eighteen months or so that preceded this book.

There aren't enough words to adequately express my gratitude. All I can say is that I hope and pray that each one of you can grab an apple box, go stand tall in the sun and then, in full view of the world, power pose like crazy. For each of you is a true superhero. You may not have saved *the* world but you did save *my* world.

Thank you:

My lit agent, Jennifer Joel at ICM, is the one who told me that my crazy personal experiment saying Yes to everything should be a book and then patiently dropped the breadcrumbs that led this crazy brain to the finish line. Marysue Rucci at Simon & Schuster hired me to write a book on motherhood and then when I discovered that I didn't want to write that book, gamely allowed me to write this book instead. I'm delighted, expanded and changed by the experience of working with her and with Jenn. That is my definition of dream job.

My TV agent, Chris Silbermann at ICM, was supportive and, instead of reminding me that I already have too many jobs and too many kids to add anything else to my plate, acted as my personal gladiator at all times. Michael Gendler is the legal brain who makes all things possible. Chris DiIorio at PMK-BNC continues his Sisyphean effort to roll the stone that is me up that hill and not once has he put my head in a box or made a suit out of my skin. Not one minute of this journey into the public eye would have been possible without him.

Ilee and Vera Rhimes are my parents. They made me. They shaped me and molded me. They endlessly indulged my need to discuss my "plan for my future" and they applauded my ambitions. My father told me "the only limit to your success is your own imagination" and my mother fixed, handled and Poped anyone who tried to make me feel this was not true. They were my very first gladiators. Every child should be raised with the same encouragement and fierce protection.

As a whole, my brothers and sisters are great people. In particular, my sister Sandie Bailey has more talents, skills and gifts than anyone I've ever known. That she uses many of them to make *my* life better is beyond wonderful. That she will tuck a baby under her arm at a moment's notice so I can write makes her awe-inspiring. That she will fiercely protect me when she thinks I can't see her *and* mock me to my face at the first sign of my self-absorption makes her perfect. That we share our singular experience of childhood together is something I would not trade for the world.

The contents of this book should make clear why I owe my sister Delorse Bond a debt of gratitude. But know that what I've told you about her in these pages is only the tip of a very large iceberg. If I told you everything she's done for me, it would take volumes. So I will just tell you that I know Delorse to be weird and wonderful and old-fashioned and nerdy and hilarious and soulful and selfless and amazing and only she will understand the depth of compliment when I say she has been for me both a Slayer and a Time Lord: *I am defended.*

Christopher Thoms is my brother from another mother. Adding him to my family was the best thing I've ever done. Our lives may change but our Cashio Street lives on.

I have three children whom I love more than anything. So I could never run Shondaland or write this book without real help at home. If I tried, we would starve and roll around in filth like pigs. In order to do what I do, I have a village of powerful, kickass working women who make my house a home. So I thank Mirtha Ross, Kelly Cheever, Ula Hrynhok,

Cassidy Brown, Taylor Thompson, Calais Brown. And I'll say it again: Jenny McCarthy is my everything. These women *save* me, and while I was writing this book they sustained me in ways I could not have dreamed.

Harper, Emerson and Beckett are quite simply the greatest, best, most special and talented, brilliant, beautiful children. No other children compare. Every single thing they do, say and are is perfect—even when it is not. They are unfolding exactly as they should and they are a constant reminder to stop and play.

Cassidy Brown read the manuscript as it came out of the printer chapter by chapter and encouraged me. Erin Cancino and Alison Eakle read the completed manuscript before anyone else and took the opportunity to tell me in detail what sucked. An honest opinion is priceless. That all three women gave theirs fearlessly restores my faith in humanity.

Abby Chambers listened to me read aloud as I typed and Zola, Gordon and Scott listened to me fret over drinks. My amazing team of assistants—Abby, Erin, Lense, Matt—kept me sane, fed and moving forward. My favorite Teamster, Mike Reynolds, parked on many a quiet side street and refused to divulge my location so I could write in peace from the back seat of the car.

Betsy Beers defies discussion. I would need to write a book about her many awesome ways. She, Pete Nowalk and every single member of my *Grey's Anatomy* family, my *Scandal* family, my *How to Get Away with Murder* family and my larger Shondaland family are gifted, enthusiastic and joyful. They make me want to go to work.

The writers in the Shondaland Writers' Rooms have provided me with camaraderie, solace, magic, intelligence, fun, baked goods, tap class, "Love, Joan," the emergency story rule (when in doubt, go vampire), gossip, arts and crafts, war stories, Scotch Tuesdays/Wine Fridays/Margarita Mondays and a whole world of incredible creative talent. Track would never be laid without them.

Linda Lowy has made my world better and more creative with her casting. I have so much gratitude for every single actor she's discovered and placed in front of me. For *this* book, I thank her most mightily for bringing Sandra Oh into my orbit.

Everyone at ABC and ABC Studios was as gracious, lovely and supportive during this book process as they have always been. They continue to make their studio a wonderful place to call home.

There are two guys deep inside Apple somewhere with very soothing phone voices who saved this manuscript and kept me from throwing myself into the ocean after I spilled a bottle of water on my MacBook Pro while writing. Thank you, Stuart and Jason, wherever you are.

Dana Asher, Cathy Highland, Verlyn Antoine are my glam team. They make me look and feel beautiful. More than that, they bring out a better me than I knew existed. I am grateful for them on a daily basis. Remember that the only reason I ever look like this when you see me is because THREE people worked a minimum of TWO AND A HALF HOURS (plus shopping, fitting, tailoring the clothes) on me. I did *not* wake up like this.

Eva Cwynar, MD, saved my life and became my friend. Your determination and belief and encouragement were and continue to be invaluable to me. There are no words to say thank you.

Gordon James, Zola Mashariki and Scott Brown are extraordinary individuals. They have rallied around me in ways I did not know possible and they taught me to redefine my idea of real friendship. The no-judgments, truth-telling, HTH nature of our fierce, dream-filled little gang of Bonnies and Clydes feels limitless. All obstacles are surmountable, every hill can be conquered. The paintings they have hung on my walls are some of the best: the dance lessons in Edgartown, the emergency Cabotties in the TV room, the Soho House brunches, the BYOB (bring your own baby) Sundays, the amazing conversations, the revelations, the fun, the fun, the fun . . . Delorse inspired me to begin but these three refused to let me quit. The road we travel together is pure hard-core Ride or Die all the way.

When I told Sandra Oh I wrote this book, I talked about overcoming the fear of speaking up for myself. She nodded because she knew how it had been for me. But still she looked puzzled.

"What," she finally asked, "did you do with something if you were too afraid to say it *before* your Year of Yes?"

I stared at her a long beat. "Sandra," I said slowly, "YOU said it for me."

Sandra blinked. "Oh. Oh! Oh, right, oh my *god.*"

We keep surprising each other with revelations. Sandra created a character with me that changed both of our lives forever in ways we are still continuing to discover. To process. To recover from. I don't think Sandra and I will ever fully understand the impact we have had on each other. The two of us are halves of one fiction and the sum of one experience. I thank her for joining me on this journey—sometimes painful, sometimes beautiful. Always educational. Forever freeing.

Cristina Yang made me brave. I thank her for appearing out of the ether.

Finally, to anyone out there who has watched any one of my shows and enjoyed it—even one episode, even one time—I am beyond grateful. It means that, at least once, I did something right.

You must do the things you think you cannot do.
—ELEANOR ROOSEVELT

Photo Credits

About the Author

Shonda Rhimes is the critically acclaimed and award-winning creator and executive producer of the hit television series *Grey's Anatomy*, *Private Practice* and *Scandal,* and the executive director of *How to Get Away with Murder*. Her writing credits also include *Princess Diaries 2: A Royal Engagement*, *Crossroads* and *Introducing Dorothy Dandridge*. Rhimes holds a BA in English Literature with Creative Writing from Dartmouth College and an MFA from the USC School of Cinema-Television as well as honorary PhDs from both institutions. Rhimes has twice been included in *TIME* magazine's list of The 100 Most Influential People along with *Fortune* magazine's 50 Most Powerful Women in Business, *Variety*'s Power of Women and *Glamour* magazine's Women of the Year. In 2013, Rhimes was appointed by President Obama to serve as trustee for the John F. Kennedy Center for the Performing Arts.

For her work on *Grey's Anatomy*, Rhimes received the 2007 Television Producer of the Year Award by the Producers Guild of America, the 2007 Golden Globe Award for Outstanding Television Drama, the 2007 Lucy Award for Excellence in Television from Women in Film, the 2006 Writers Guild Award for Best New Series, in addition to Emmy nominations for Outstanding Drama Series and Writing for a Drama Series. For *Scandal*, Rhimes was the 2013 winner of the prestigious Peabody Award. Rhimes was the recipient of the 2012 GLAAD Golden Gate Award, the 2010 RAINN Hope Award and the 2010 and 2011 Television Academy Honors Awards. Rhimes was the 2005, 2013 and 2014 winner of the AFI Award for Television Program of the Year. In addition, Rhimes has won six NAACP Image Awards for Outstanding Writing in a Dramatic Series as well as eight NAACP Image Awards for Outstanding Drama Series.

In 2014, Rhimes and producing partner Betsy Beers received the Directors Guild of America's prestigious Diversity Award. This marked only the fifth time the organization had bestowed this award. Rhimes was additionally a 2014 recipient of the W. E. B. Du Bois Medal from Harvard, the Sherry Lansing Leadership Award from *The Hollywood Reporter* and was named to both the 2014 New Establishment List for *Vanity Fair* and the New Guard List of 50 Most Connected Women in America for *Marie Claire*. In 2015, Rhimes was awarded the Paddy Chayefsky

Laurel Award for Television Writing Achievement from the Writers Guild of America, West, and was inducted into the Broadcasting Hall of Fame by the National Association of Broadcasters. She was also bestowed the Eleanor Roosevelt Global Women's Rights Award from the Feminist Majority Foundation in recognition of her work in changing the face of media.

Born and raised in Chicago, IL, Rhimes now lives in Shondaland, a very real and very imagined place that could be somewhere inside Los Angeles. She's the proud mother of three daughters.

ml   12-7-